Seeking God

with
Saint John
Henry Newman

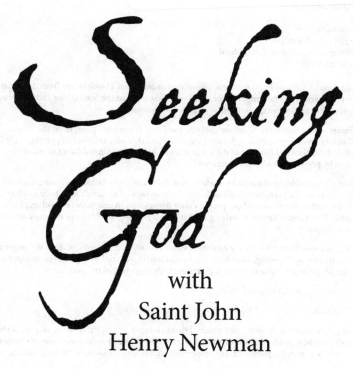

RYAN J. MARR

Our Sunday Visitor
Huntington, Indiana

Nihil Obstat
Msgr. Michael Heintz, Ph.D.
Censor Librorum

Imprimatur
✠ Kevin C. Rhoades
Bishop of Fort Wayne-South Bend
June 22, 2020

The *Nihil Obstat* and *Imprimatur* are official declarations that a book is free from doctrinal or moral error. It is not implied that those who have granted the *Nihil Obstat* and *Imprimatur* agree with the contents, opinions, or statements expressed.

Every reasonable effort has been made to determine copyright holders of excerpted materials and to secure permissions as needed. If any copyrighted materials have been inadvertently used in this work without proper credit being given in one form or another, please notify Our Sunday Visitor in writing so that future printings of this work may be corrected accordingly.

In quotations from John Henry Newman, some alterations have been made to the original punctuation and spelling, so as to bring the text into closer conformity with contemporary rules of grammar. None of these changes affects the meaning of the quotations.

Our Sunday Visitor Publishing Division
Our Sunday Visitor, Inc.
200 Noll Plaza
Huntington, IN 46750
www.osv.com
1-800-348-2440

ISBN: 978-1-68192-592-9 (Inventory No.T2457)
1. RELIGION—Christianity—Catholic.
2. RELIGION—Christianity—Saints & Sainthood.
3. RELIGION—Christian Life—Spiritual Growth.

eISBN: 978-1-68192-593-6
LCCN: 2020939150

Cover, interior design: Chelsea Alt
Cover art: Bridgeman Images
Interior design: Chelsea Alt

PRINTED IN THE UNITED STATES OF AMERICA

For Catharine M. Ryan and Father Drew Morgan, without whose support this project would not have been possible.

ABBREVIATIONS

Apo.	Apologia Pro Vita Sua
AW	Autobiographical Writings
DA	Discussions and Arguments on Various Subjects
Dev.	An Essay on the Development of Christian Doctrine
Ess. i, ii	Essays, Critical and Historical
GA	An Essay in Aid of a Grammar of Assent
Jfc.	Lectures on the Doctrine of Justification
LD	The Letters and Diaries of John Henry Newman
MD	Meditations and Devotions of the Late Cardinal Newman
Mix.	Discourses Addressed to Mixed Congregations
OS	Sermons Preached on Various Occasions
PS i–viii	Parochial and Plain Sermons, 8 vols.
SD	Sermons Bearing on Subjects of the Day
US	Fifteen Sermons Preached before the University of Oxford
VV	Verses on Various Occasions

ABBREVIATIONS

Contents

Contents

INTRODUCTION

NEWMAN AS SPIRITUAL GUIDE ON THE PATH TO HOLINESS

Life is fleeting! The biblical authors warn us as much. The Letter of James, for example, summarizes the human condition in particularly stark terms: "What is your life? For you are a mist that appears for a little time and then vanishes" (4:14). The psalmist drives this same point home, comparing mortals to the flowers of the field: they flourish for a time, but then the wind passes over them, and they are gone, never to be known again (see Ps 103:15–16). Time marches steadily onward, and if we are not careful, we can reach the end of our days only to find that we have wasted our time pursuing meaningless things.

We all want our lives to matter — to have some sort of lasting significance. But this can prove elusive, even for those who have the best of intentions. Think back, for instance, on the past ten to fifteen years of your life. If you are anything like me, there are many things that, with the wisdom you have now, you would have done differently. Yet, here you are today — your past frozen, as it were — living with the consequences of the decisions that have brought you to this point. I've heard more than one older acquaintance remark that "youth is wasted on the young." For whatever reason, as human beings, we don't seem to realize how precious time is until it's gone. But once time has slipped through our hands, there is no recovering it. Life can be lived only forward; there are no mulligans.

This is one of the reasons why it's so important to find a trusted spiritual director — someone who is able to see shortcomings in our character that we are prone to overlook and who can help us to avoid pitfalls that might hamper our spiritual progress. And it's not only young people who suffer from shortsightedness and willfulness. The human heart is incredibly prone to self-deception, such that good intentions, on their own, are rarely enough to keep us on the right path. Even the saints testify to the need for a good spiritual director. Saint Faustina, for example, once admitted, "If only I had had a spiritual director from the beginning, then I would not have wasted so many of God's graces."[1] A good director, Faustina added, "knows how to avoid the rocks against which the soul could be shattered."[2] Saint John Henry Newman had a similar outlook, noting that "we should all of us be saved a great deal of suffering of various kinds, if we could but persuade ourselves that we are not the best judges, whether of our own condition, or of God's will towards us. What sensible person undertakes to be his own physician? Yet are the diseases of the mind less numerous, less intricate, less subtle than those of the body?"[3] Long story short, we can spare ourselves a lot of potential heartache by turning to a trustworthy spiritual adviser.

As a supplement to (not as a replacement for!) a living spiritual director, we can also invite into our lives holy figures of the past who offer a different kind of guidance through the memory of their witness. These are almost always saints, holy men and women whose writings have been identified by the Church as theologically sound and devotionally fruitful. Certainly, there is much to be gained by sitting across from a director who can provide a listening ear and immediate feedback. It's also true, though, that we are unlikely to find a spiritual director who has attained the level of sanctity that was evident in the lives of such figures as Saint Thérèse of Lisieux or Saint Francis de Sales. Ultimately, it's unnecessary to pit one method against the other. We should all seek out a spiritual director with whom we can meet on a regular basis, while seeking to learn as much as we can from the lives of the saints since we know that they were filled with the Holy Spirit in a profound way.

The book you hold in your hands is an invitation to receive spiritual direction from one of the towering Catholic intellectuals of the nineteenth century: Saint John Henry Newman. Now, if you are worried that this book is going to be overly intellectual or impractical, I encourage you to stick with me, for Newman was much more than a thinker. He was a man of deep prayer, who exuded personal holiness and had a compassionate, priestly heart for those who came under his pastoral care. Newman's thirty-one volumes of letters, many of them written to parishioners who sought out his counsel, are a monument to the far-reaching impact of his priestly ministry, and the concerns of this ministry remained always at the forefront of his thoughts. Certainly, Newman's intellectual gifts were immense, but for him, they mattered only insofar as he was helping others to grow in faith, hope, and love.

Newman was also one of the finest preachers of his day, and his sermons have produced thousands of conversions, some of these during his lifetime and many more in the intervening years since his death. His body of sermons contains a rich treasure of spiritual insights, and reflection on their content makes up the bulk of this book. A recurring theme in those sermons is the urgency of setting aside our selfish desires in order to do God's will. In one of his most convicting treatments of this topic, "God's Will the End of Life," Newman contrasts what God wills for us with the way the vast majority of people live. He notes that, if you peer into the lives of most modern persons, you will find an underlying lukewarmness when it comes to the things of God. Many of us "do not bargain to be rich or to be great; but we do bargain, whether rich or poor, high or low, to live for ourselves, to live for the lust of the moment, or, according to the doctrine of the hour, thinking of the future and the unseen just as much or as little as we please."[4]

Notice, here, that Newman does not focus on grave wrong-doings but highlights a far more common spiritual malaise, that of apathy or lack of attention to spiritual realities. For many of us, our sins will never be the stuff of tell-all biographies. The greater danger, rather, is that we will be lulled to sleep by the comforts of this life, mistaking material comfort for a sign of divine approval and viewing the sacrifices that Christ calls us to make as either unnecessary or, worse, as an intrusion upon the life that "*I* have made for *myself.*" Newman says it is a "shocking thought" to consider that "the multitude of men are living without any aim beyond this visible scene."[5] From a spiritual vantage point, so many of us are like frogs swimming in a pot of water that is slowly being brought to a boil. Even though our well-being is becoming more precarious by the moment, we fail to recognize it because we have become so accustomed to our surroundings, and we figure that things will always remain just as they are right now. Newman's writings, if one takes the time to meditate upon them, can serve as a much-needed wake-up call for those of us who might be prone to approaching life on those terms. Saint John Henry Newman has had an enormous impact on my faith, and my goal in these pages is to channel just a fraction of his wisdom for the sake of others who might be looking for a charge to their spiritual lives.

HOW TO READ THIS BOOK

To get the most out of this book, you will want to maintain as reference points two mottoes that Newman adopted as guiding principles in his life. The first is "Life is for action." For Newman, this motto was a reminder that to accomplish great things, we sometimes have to venture beyond what we can prove at any given time. Our culture tends to value skepticism. It's commonly asserted that one should not accept as true what cannot be proven with absolute certainty. Newman, however, recognized that if we waited until every intellectual hurdle was cleared away before we acted, we would never accomplish anything: "Life is not long enough for a religion of inferences," he wrote; "we shall never have done beginning, if we determine to begin with proof. We shall ever be laying our foundations. ... Life is for action. If we insist on proofs for everything, we shall never come to action: to act you must assume, and that assumption is faith."[6] Here I must address a possible misunderstanding. When Newman mentions being motivated by faith, he does not have in mind taking a blind leap or acting contrary to reason. Faith is not unreasonable, but neither can it be constrained within the limitations of reason. When it comes to following God's call, sometimes we are forced to act prior to having all of our difficulties resolved, and then it is only after acting — after practicing obedience — that the reasons of faith begin to make sense to us.

As Newman says, "Ten thousand difficulties do not [add up to] one doubt."[7] Though it's important to struggle with the difficulties that faith raises for us, they need not, should not, prevent us from acting or cause us to descend into a hopeless state of doubt. Again, life is for action. To accomplish great things, we must make "ventures of faith ... [yet] without the absolute certainty of success."[8] Newman continues: "This, indeed, is the very meaning of the word 'venture;' for that is a strange venture which has nothing in it of fear, risk, danger, anxiety, uncertainty."[9] So, as you read this book, if you find yourself struggling with doubts or anxiety, keep in mind Newman's counsel. Resolve not to allow doubts or fear of failure to prevent you from a venture of faith, "for nothing would be done at all, if [we] waited till [we] could do it so well that no one could find fault with it."[10] Like Abraham, we have to be willing to journey to an unfamiliar place if we are to discover all that God has prepared for us to accomplish. If Newman's spiritual wisdom is going to bear fruit in your life, you must be willing to act on the convictions that well up within you before you necessarily see the whole picture.

Another motto that Newman adopted and held dear was "Holiness before peace." On the surface, this second motto can appear confusing. Are not holiness and peace both vital aspects of life in Christ? Why prioritize one (holiness) over the other (peace)? To understand what Newman had in mind with this motto, we have to grasp precisely how he was using the term "peace." "Peace" can refer to a fruit of the spirit (see Gal 5:22). This kind of peace is always good and should be pursued by all Christians, regardless of their circumstances. "Have no anxiety about anything," Paul exhorts the Christians at Philippi, "but in everything by prayer and supplication with thanksgiving let your requests be made known to God. And the peace of God, which passes all understanding, will keep your hearts and your minds in Christ Jesus" (Phil 4:6–7). Supernatural peace is promised to us in Scripture, so when this peace is lacking, we should renew our efforts to cast all of our anxiety upon God (see 1 Pt 5:7).

But there is another way that we use the word "peace," and that is as "the absence of conflict." While acknowledging that Christians are called to live at peace with their neighbors, Newman also saw that the desire for peace can sometimes be used as an excuse for avoiding necessary conflict. For example, we may remain quiet about our faith in certain circles because we fear losing friends who do not share our convictions. Or perhaps we cut corners at work and sacrifice our integrity for the sake of keeping a job. In such instances, we are opting for "peace" — the absence of conflict — over holiness.

Of course, we have to be prudent in deciding when and how to witness to the Gospel. I have met some Christians who assume that they are being persecuted like the prophets just because others happen not to like them.[11] This is a mistaken mindset: We shouldn't go out of our way to step on others' toes. But we should recognize that being faithful to what God is calling us to will inevitably involve some level of conflict with the power brokers of this world. As Our Lord said to his disciples, "If the world hates you, keep in mind that it hated me first. If you belonged to the world, it would love you as its own. As it is, you do not belong to the world, but I have chosen you out of the world. That is why the world hates you" (Jn 15:18–19, NIV). Newman makes a similar point in his sermon "The Ventures of Faith," in which he challenges his listeners to take risks that might cost them something for the kingdom of God. In Newman's view, more of the Church's members need to develop "a high and unearthly spirit," such as the saints have.[12] "How is it," he asks, "that we are so contented with things as they are — that we are so willing to be let alone, and to enjoy this life — that we make such excuses, if any one presses on us the necessity of something higher, the duty of bearing the Cross, if we would earn the Crown, of the Lord Jesus Christ?"[13]

Newman's description of those who want "to be let alone and to enjoy this life" really gets to the heart of the matter. This outlook, unfortunately, has broken out like a plague during several periods in Christian history. Consider, for instance, how many millions of baptized Christians lived in Germany when the Nazis rose to power, yet only a tiny minority spoke out against the heinous actions that were perpetrated by the Third Reich. And while it may be easy to disparage the apathy and silence of German Christians from that era, who knows for sure what sorts of things future generations might chastise us for failing to speak out against. In this light, if our lives are devoid of conflict or if we feel little or no tension over the predominant values of the broader culture, we may want to reevaluate the substance of our witness.

With the above in mind, we could repurpose another maxim from Newman's preaching: "True faith is not shown here below in peace, but rather in conflict."[14] Now, in saying this, Newman was talking about internal conflict, or the personal struggle against sin that each Christian must wage. But his sentiment could just as aptly be applied to our public witness. As long as we are in this world, our faith will be demonstrated through conflict. The members of Christ's Body on earth are described as the Church Militant for good reason. Certainly, we ought to remember that "our battle is not against flesh and blood, but against the rulers, against the authorities, against the powers of this dark world and against the spiritual forces of evil in the heavenly realms" (Eph 6:12, NIV, slightly altered). Battle we must, though, for peace gained at the expense of holiness, as Newman reminds us, is really no peace at all.

THE PRAYERFUL READER

One final caveat: As you read this book, it's essential that you be regularly engaged in the practice of prayer, if you are not so engaged already. In one of his sermons, Newman remarks that prayer is to the spiritual life what the beating of the heart is to the life of the body. Reading about holiness without consistently turning to God in prayer is like trying to travel somewhere in a vehicle that has no fuel in it. Spiritual reading, on its own, will get you nowhere. We must be persons of prayer!

If you long for a deeper prayer life but are not sure where to begin, a great resource is Newman's *Meditations and Devotions*, a collection of devotional reflections and prayers that were culled from his personal papers after he died.[15] This thin volume packs a powerful punch and will help you to experience for yourself the very spiritual insights that we will be discussing from Newman's sermons. As we begin this journey together, please know that I am praying for you, confident as well that Newman is praying for all of us who are still traveling "along the way." In closing, then, I offer the following prayer by Newman as a benediction for the journey that lies ahead of us:

> But for us, let us glory in what [the children of this age] disown; let us beg of our Divine Lord to take to Him His great power, and manifest Himself more and more, and reign both in our hearts and in the world. Let us beg of Him to stand by us in trouble, and guide us on our dangerous way. May He, as of old, choose "the foolish things of the world to confound the wise, and the weak things of the world to confound the things which are mighty!" May He support us all the day long, till the shades lengthen, and the evening comes, and the busy world is hushed, and the fever of life is over, and our work is done! Then in His mercy may He give us safe lodging, and a holy rest, and peace at the last! [Amen.][16]

1

HIGHLIGHTS FROM NEWMAN'S LIFE

When I visited the Birmingham Oratory for the first time, I was struck by, among other things, the littleness and simplicity of Saint John Henry Newman's living quarters. Here, in a relatively obscure town — far away from the corridors of wealth and power — a slight, unassuming priest exercised an extraordinary influence on an untold number of lives, accomplishing most of what he did through work done in a single room of a modest priestly residence. In the case of Saint John Henry, the biblical adage rings powerfully true: God truly does use the weak things of this world to shame the strong (see 1 Cor 1:27).

The witness of Newman turns on its head the way we commonly think about how the world works. Modern Westerners tend to view public life through the lens of coercive power. To have an impact on society, to make a name for oneself, to accomplish anything great, one must hold worldly influence and wield it ruthlessly. It is a dog-eat-dog world, we tell ourselves, and the vast majority of the human race can be moved only by the threat of punishment or the loss of privilege.

Saint John Henry refused to approach life according to these terms. While others sought prestige, he chose the lowly path, and in his sermons he consistently counseled his listeners to practice humility and self-denial rather than to insist upon their rights and privileges. Ultimately, Newman recognized where true power resides. He took Christ at his word that, if we will have faith even as small as a mustard seed, we will be able to move mountains (see Mt 17:20). Through his preaching, his writing, and his spiritual counsel, Newman moved something more imposing than mountains: he moved hearts, thousands of them, and, in so doing, he left an indelible impact on the Catholic Church in England.

In his time, Newman was an accomplished scholar, poet, educator, novelist, and philosopher. A thorough treatment of any one of these facets of his life could easily fill hundreds of pages. Our purpose in this book, however, is to zero in on Newman's life of heroic virtue in order to glean insights that might aid our journey to God. We will walk the path that Newman trod and listen to his recounting of what that journey involved, so that we ourselves might grow in holiness — with the ultimate goal of attaining the union with God that Newman already knows in full. In this book, then, we will be seeking God *with* John Henry Newman. As numerous Catholics can attest, there are few more reliable guides on the path of life than this saintly convert and kindly priest, who continues to draw many hearts to God some 130 years after his death.

THE LIFE OF NEWMAN

At the beatification ceremony for Blessed Dominic Barberi — the Italian Passionist priest who received Newman into the Catholic Church — Pope Paul VI took time in his address to touch briefly upon the enduring legacy of Newman. Specifically, the pope described Newman as one who, "guided solely by love of the truth and fidelity to Christ, traced an itinerary, the most toilsome, but also the greatest, the most meaningful, the most conclusive, that human thought ever travelled during the [nineteenth] century, indeed one might say during the modern era, to arrive at the fullness of wisdom and of peace."[17] Paul VI's remarks memorably encapsulate the dramatic character of Newman's arduous spiritual journey, which could succinctly be described as an unwavering search for the truth.

When Newman was born, on February 21, 1801, no one could have predicted that this infant would eventually become the greatest English-speaking Roman Catholic theologian of his time. Newman was born to practicing, though not overly zealous, Anglican parents — John and Jemima Newman (neé Fourdrinier). For our purposes, it's unnecessary to dwell at length upon the details of John Henry's childhood, except to note that there was nothing noticeably unconventional about his upbringing. Newman's religious formation was largely in the mode of "Bible Religion" — a term that he used later in his life to describe "the national religion of England."[18] This way of practicing the Faith revolved around devotional reading of the Bible, both in a communal setting in church and privately at home. Whatever limitations there may have been to this approach, the Bible-centered religion of Newman's youth would have a lifelong impact on his witness to the Gospel, as evidenced perhaps most markedly in the way that his sermons are saturated with the language of Sacred Scripture.

As a young man, Newman enrolled at Trinity College, Oxford. His time as a student was a mixed bag: Although he thoroughly enjoyed the intellectual stimulation of university life, he did not fit in socially, largely on account of his unwillingness to participate in the drinking bouts that occupied his peers. Social ostracization at the college had its advantages, however, in that Newman had ample time to study. Unfortunately, his studiousness backfired on him in 1821, when he drove himself to the brink of a mental breakdown by overpreparing for his examinations. As a result, he fared poorly on the exams, ending up off the honors list for mathematics and in the lower division of the second class — or "under the line" — for classics. Feeling himself an embarrassment to his family, Newman feared that his hopes for a fellowship at Oxford had been lost. In April of 1822, however, he received the surprising news that he had been elected a fellow of Oriel College. Apparently, Newman's intellectual prowess as manifested in his written work had outweighed any concerns raised by his performance on the exams.

Newman later described his earning this fellowship as "the turning point of his life,"[19] but it could just as aptly be considered a key turning point in the history of the Church of England. For it was during his time as a fellow at Oriel that Newman became the de facto leader of the Oxford movement. This was an effort led by several key Oxford figures to return the Church of England to its Catholic roots, by integrating some pre-Reformation devotional and liturgical traditions into contemporary Anglican practice. The Oxford movement leaders also mounted a protest against the incursion of state authority in the decision-making of the Church. In their view, the Church as an apostolic community was accountable to God alone. Permitting the state to have any role in ecclesiastical governance was, for them, a compromise of the Church's fundamental identity. Newman and his Oxford movement confrères disseminated their ideas through a series of pamphlets, or *Tracts for the Times*, which is how they came to be known as Tractarians.

For a time, the Tractarians made significant headway in bringing about the reforms they sought, but eventually Newman lost his zeal for this effort — in part because of the negative reaction to one of his published tracts (Tract 90), but even more significantly because he started to doubt his conviction that the Church of England was truly catholic and apostolic. During the 1830s, Newman had pressed the argument that Anglicanism struck a *via media* between the errors of Protestantism on one side, and the excesses of Romanism on the other. At this stage in his life, Newman claimed that the Church of England was apostolic because it held fast to the creedal commitments of the early Church. In his view, Protestant communities neglected key parts of the apostolic tradition, while Roman Catholicism added to it. However, certain developments in the late 1830s — including the Church of England's decision to share a bishopric in Jerusalem with Lutherans — caused Newman to reconsider the whole question of where the one Church of Christ could be found.[20] Over the next few years, his doubts accelerated, such that by 1841 Newman was on his "deathbed" regarding his membership in the Anglican Church.[21]

The following year, Newman withdrew with some of his closest friends to Littlemore, outside Oxford, where he and this circle of followers began to practice a form of life that closely resembled traditional monasticism. On September 25, 1843, he preached his last Anglican sermon, "The Parting of Friends," at the quaint parish church he had designed in Littlemore. Two years later, on October 9, 1845, he was received into the Roman Catholic Church by Father Dominic Barberi, who was serving during that time as a missionary in England. Newman said his entry into the Catholic Church was "like coming into port after a rough sea."[22] Despite undergoing many personal trials in the years that followed, he never regretted his decision to swim the Tiber.

NEWMAN'S CATHOLIC YEARS

As intimated in the previous section, Newman's time as a Roman Catholic was characterized by a series of personal difficulties and professional disappointments. Newman began seminary studies in Rome in the fall of 1846, before being ordained to the Catholic priesthood on May 30, 1847. After a period of ministry in England, he relocated to Dublin in 1854 to serve as the first rector of the newly established Catholic University of Ireland, only to resign from that position a few years later, on account of the stress that he was experiencing and also because he sensed that the Irish bishops were not fully supportive of his vision for the institution.

At the end of that decade, Newman found himself increasingly under the microscope of the English hierarchy due to an article that he had written recommending that bishops consult the lay faithful on matters of doctrine. Bishop Brown of Newport even went so far as to report Newman to Roman authorities on suspicion of heresy — a charge that wasn't completely cleared up until several years later. Newman also had to fight a frivolous lawsuit leveled against him by a corrupt ex-priest, lost his closest friend to an early death, and regularly butted heads with the primate of England — his sometime friend and fellow convert Archbishop Henry Manning.

The list could go on, and things got so bad that, for a time, many Englanders wondered whether Newman would return to the religious communion of his youth. When Newman got wind of this rumor, he squashed it forcefully, writing that he had never "had one moment's wavering of trust in the Catholic Church since [being] received into her fold" and adding that he had still "an unclouded faith in her creed in all its articles; a supreme satisfaction in her worship, discipline, and teaching; and an eager longing and a hope against hope that the many dear friends whom I have left in Protestantism may be partakers of my happiness."[23] For Newman, the Catholic Church was first and foremost a gracious gift given by God in order to bring us salvation, but she also exists, he believed, to sustain us through the storms of life. To commit oneself to life in the Church, therefore, is part of what it means to practice trust in God's providential care.

This abandonment to Divine Providence that Newman practiced constantly informed his thought about life in the Church and, in turn, the counsel that he gave to others regarding how to live as members of the Body of Christ. As an example, we can look at how Newman navigated the events surrounding the First Vatican Council (1869–1870), which was an exceedingly trying time for him. At this council, a certain group of bishops sought to ratify a strongly worded statement regarding the pope's power to teach infallibly (i.e., without error) on matters of faith and morals. In their view, such a definition would reinforce the Church's teaching authority and thus help to protect Catholics against the winds of philosophical skepticism that were sweeping across Europe in the nineteenth century.

Since becoming Catholic, Newman had believed in the pope's infallibility as a theological opinion. Nevertheless, he thought that this group of bishops was acting recklessly by insisting on a strongly worded definition without giving due attention to the complexities of Church history and without showing sufficient concern for the consciences of those who had difficulty with the idea. In short, Newman thought the Church needed more time to work out a definition of the doctrine that clearly specified the limits of infallibility in light of certain historical instances that appeared to stand in tension with the idea — for instance, the fact that a few popes had privately held theological convictions that were later condemned by the Church.

When the bishops at Vatican I ended up approving a definition of papal infallibility, Newman said that he was pleased with its moderation. He believed that the extreme party had not gotten its way but that the Holy Spirit had again guided the Church in her deliberation over a disputed theological question. Though Newman was relieved, in the years following Vatican I numerous friends and acquaintances looked to him for counsel as they struggled to make sense of the definition and its implications. And this gets to the key point for our purposes. Rather than dismissing their concerns, Newman encouraged these individuals to turn to God when they were troubled in conscience by what they were witnessing in the Church. In an 1871 letter to Alfred Plummer, for instance, Newman wrote:

> Another consideration has struck me forcibly, and
> that is, that, looking at early history, it would seem
> as if the Church moved on to the perfect truth by
> various successive declarations, alternately in con-
> trary directions, and thus perfecting, completing,

supplying each other. Let us have a little faith in
her, I say. Pius [IX] is not the last of the Popes —
the fourth Council modified the third, the fifth,
the fourth. ... *Let us be patient, let us have faith,* and
a new Pope, and a re-assembled Council may trim
the boat.[24]

In other words, God has guided the Church this far amid
many ferocious storms, and we can trust that God will continue
to guide her in the years to come. Our belief in the indefectibility
of the Church — i.e., that the gates of hell will not prevail against
her (see Mt 16:18) — does not rest on the greatness of our strength,
or on the natural gifts of our bishops, but solely on the promises of
God. It is God who preserves the Church, and thus, we should seek
to have the kind of patience that Newman recommends whenever
we find ourselves disturbed by the circumstances around us.

As for our own experience of the Church, today we are less
likely to fret over such issues as papal infallibility or the political
machinations that took place at Vatican I, but, for different reasons, it can still be difficult to live as a member of the Body of
Christ. Alongside the challenge of intellectually making sense of
the Faith, contemporary Catholics may struggle with the hypoc-
risy that we see in the Church or with the abuse perpetrated by
some who were appointed to be our pastors. Regardless of which
factors cause you to question your faith, Newman's example can
serve as a source of inspiration. Newman dealt with heavy-handed
bishops, and at times he was troubled by the narrow-mindedness
that he perceived on the part of certain outspoken Catholics.[25] But
he never contemplated leaving the Church. Besides his sense that
God was ultimately in control, Newman was also convinced that
Christianity was inherently a social religion. In terms of living out
the Faith, then, there are no Lone Ranger disciples. We come to
know the love of God not in spite of but precisely through our
communion with our brothers and sisters in Christ. As Newman
once observed, "the love of our private friends is the only prepa-

ratory exercise for the love of all men."[26] And there is no more intimate form of friendship, arguably, than walking together as baptized members of Christ's Body. Life in the Church is far from perfect, but by remaining committed to the family of God, we will learn to sacrifice our selfish desires in humble submission to others who are themselves imperfect.

Newman did not merely preach these ideas; he also modeled them — most notably, in his leadership of the Oratory community of priests that he established in Birmingham. Since its founding in 1849, the Birmingham Oratory has been a shining testimony to Newman's theology of friendship, which is rooted in shared worship of the Triune God. From Newman's vantage point, the love we have for our friends and our relationship to God are inextricably bound together. As 1 John 4:20 warns, "If any one says, 'I love God,' and hates his brother, he is a liar; for he who does not love his brother whom he has seen, cannot love God whom he has not seen." In a similar vein, Newman wrote:

> Should God call upon us to preach to the world, surely we must obey His call; but at present, let us do what lies before us. Little children, let us love one another. Let us be meek and gentle; let us think before we speak; let us try to improve our talents in private life; let us do good, not hoping for a return, and avoiding all display before men. Well may I so exhort you at this [Christmas] season, when we have so lately partaken together the Blessed Sacrament which binds us to mutual love, and gives us strength to practice it. Let us not forget the promise we then made, or the grace we then received. We are not our own; we are bought with the blood of Christ; we are consecrated to be temples of the Holy Spirit, an unutterable privilege, which is weighty enough to sink us with shame at our unworthiness, did it not the while

strengthen us by the aid itself imparts, to bear its extreme costliness.[27]

Newman's pastoral heart shines forth brightly in this exhortation. For him, heeding the call of God meant, first and foremost, embodying a life of meekness, mutual love, and unassuming beneficence toward others. By following this "little way," Newman did end up "preach[ing] to the world," but he did not start with this latter accomplishment in view. He began with friendship and humble service to others and then trusted God to multiply the fruits of these small offerings, and God clearly did.

In 1890, after nearly seven decades of humble service in the kingdom of God, Newman passed away after a brief bout with pneumonia. In his will, Newman had made provisions for a small memorial plaque to be installed at the Oratory, upon which were inscribed the words *Ex umbris et imaginibus in veritatem* — "Out of shadows and images into truth." After a lifetime of seeking the truth, Newman had finally reached his home, the loving embrace of his heavenly Father. The epitaph that Newman chose for his funerary marker was eventually incorporated into the collect for his feast day; it is a moving prayer that can be offered for a variety of intentions, but especially when asking for the grace to imitate his example:

> O God, who bestowed on the Priest Saint John Henry Newman the grace to follow your kindly light and find peace in your Church; graciously grant that, through his intercession and example, we may be led out of shadows and images into the fulness of your truth. Through our Lord Jesus Christ, your Son, who lives and reigns with you in the unity of the Holy Spirit, one God, for ever and ever.[28]

2

THE THREE STAGES OF THE SPIRITUAL LIFE

Over the centuries, great saints and mystics of the Church have mapped out a specific path for disciples to follow in order to reach God. Specifically, they have spoken of three stages in the journey toward eternal beatitude. These are the *purgative* way, the *illuminative* way, and the *unitive* way. The Christian life, then, begins with purgation (the purgative way): we must be purged of our sinful desires and disordered attachments before we are able to see God as he truly is. As these sinful desires are slowly burned away, and as we immerse ourselves in the liturgical life of the Church,[29] our knowledge of God expands (the illuminative way) — and this knowledge, in turn, elicits a burning desire to be united with our Creator and Lord. The end result of this process, the saints tell us, is loving union with God (the unitive way), which is simply another way of describing the eternal state of blessedness prepared for those who, by grace, persevere in the face of life's trials and tribulations.[30]

As far as I know, Saint John Henry Newman nowhere explicitly uses the language of the purgative, illuminative, and unitive ways. Nevertheless, these basic concepts are there, behind his various reflections on the Christian life, even if they are not directly mentioned. Though it may be impossible to determine just how much Newman had studied this stream of tradition, at the very least, the threefold path envisioned by the saints provides a helpful framework for looking at how Newman thought about striving for holiness. In this chapter, we will walk through these three stages of the spiritual life in order to draw out insights from Newman about each one.

STAGE ONE: THE PURGATIVE WAY

As a pastor of souls, Newman was well aware of the human propensity to shrink from the burning fire of God's love. Admittedly, the life of discipleship is difficult, and when faced with the arduous task of being "new-made," many of us seek to negotiate terms with God, whereby we can enjoy the benefits of salvation without having to give up everything we presently possess. We "wish to be saved," Newman writes, "but in [our] own way ... to capitulate upon terms," so as "to carry off [our] goods with [us]."[31] When we approach God in this manner, we are, in fact, deceiving ourselves. We might think our longing is for heaven, but if that were really the case, we would desire nothing but God. To approach God with terms — i.e., "I will submit to your will *if* I am allowed to keep this or that other good" — is a clear sign that one is not totally ready to experience the fullness of divine love.

One of the main causes of being tripped up in this way is the lie, which we often tell ourselves, that to turn our lives completely over to God would mean forfeiting some essential part of our identity or losing access to some pleasure or earthly enjoyment by which happiness could be found. In diagnosing this spiritual condition, Newman casts a bright light on the excuses that many of us make in refusing God's grace: "We do not like to be new-made; we are afraid of it ... and much as we profess in general terms to wish to be changed, when it comes to the point when particular instances of change are presented to us, we shrink from them, and are content to remain unchanged."[32] As Newman indicates, there is a vast difference between professing to desire union with God and actually undergoing the transformation that makes it possible. To experience the kind of change that prepares us for heaven requires passing through a fire that is painful, yes, though one that exists for the sake of our highest good. The purgative process, then, is a gift of God's grace — the divinely ordained means by which we attain "to the whole measure of the fullness of Christ" (Eph 4:13, NIV).[33]

The process of purgation, Newman suggests, ordinarily begins with very small measures. In fact, we can sometimes go off track by wanting to start at the end point — with perfection — when, in fact, holiness is "the result of a continual struggle — not spontaneous nature, but habitual self-command."[34] We may admire the stigmata of Saint Francis or the courage of the holy martyrs, but we deceive ourselves if we think that we can begin where they ended. In reality, what brought these heroic saints to that stage in their spiritual lives were many small acts of self-denial in the days and years leading up to the extraordinary events for which they are now remembered. A similar path is marked out for each one of us, and there is something spiritually dangerous about longing for a dramatic occurrence that will expedite the process. Rather than setting out to accomplish heroic deeds that will be noticed by others, we should focus our attention on "perform[ing] well the ordinary duties of the day."[35] As Newman warns his listeners in a sermon on maintaining a consistent prayer life: "It is very easy to be religious by fits and starts, and to keep up our feelings by artificial stimulants; but regularity seems to trammel us, and we become impatient."[36] If we want to gauge our progress in the spiritual life, we should not look for miraculous signs and wonders but should ask ourselves if we are practicing self-denial in the small duties that providence has ordained for us and bearing patiently the petty annoyances that the circumstances of life inevitably bring our way.

Newman's thoughts on this topic can serve as a proverbial splash of cold water for those of us who have unwittingly fallen into a spiritual slumber. As Ian Ker has noted, Newman's preaching evinces a "stark, even harsh, realism."[37] When it comes to the spiritual life, Newman refuses to peddle sentimental platitudes. His spiritual counsel, instead, is concrete and realistic, in that he targets matters of life that all of us must confront. Consider, for instance, the following litany of recommendations that Newman gives for achieving growth in the Christian life:

> Turn from ambitious thoughts, and (as far as you religiously may) make resolves against taking on you authority and rule. ... Sell [what you have] and give alms. ... Hate to spend money on yourself. Shut your ears to praise, when it grows loud. ... Curb your tongue, and turn away your eye. ... Be up at prayer "a great while before day," and seek the true, your only Bridegroom, "by night on your bed." So shall self-denial become natural to you, and a change come over you, gently and imperceptibly.[38]

As a longtime minister to persons from a range of backgrounds, Newman possessed a keen sense of the fickleness of the human heart. He knew that Satan usually trips us up not by making us think that sanctity is unheroic but by distracting us from fulfilling our ordinary duties or by convincing us that the small mortifications necessary for holiness are somehow below us. If the evil one can prevent us from being faithful in little things, we will never move on to the greatness of total conformity to Christ.

SUFFERING IN THE CHRISTIAN LIFE

When it comes to the purgative process, there are two main ways in which we can be purged of disordered attachments. The first and most obvious way, of course, is by practicing self-denial, such as fasting, almsgiving, intentional silence, and so forth. The second way is, in a certain sense, more immediate to us but can be tougher to accept, and that is through meritorious suffering. The difficulty of this second means of purgation is that suffering normally comes to us uninvited, as it were, and in and of itself has no spiritual benefit. Newman wants to make sure that his readers recognize this point:

> Now, as to its effect upon the mind, let it be well understood that [suffering] has no sanctifying influence in itself. Bad men are made worse by it. This should be borne in mind, lest we deceive ourselves; for sometimes we speak ... as though present hardship and suffering were in some sense a ground of confidence in themselves as to our future prospects, whether as expiating our sins or bringing our hearts nearer to God.[39]

No, this much is clear: many persons suffer greatly and — as far as we can tell — gain no spiritual benefit from the experience. The very fact of suffering guarantees nothing, and we deceive ourselves if we gauge our standing before God solely on the basis of the level of hardships that we face. Something additional has to be part of the suffering in order for the experience to be meritorious.

And here Newman turns to Scripture to explain what redemptive suffering looks like. The salvific work of Christ, Newman notes, was unique: Jesus' suffering "only was our Atonement; no one shared in the work."[40] And yet, mysteriously, God enables us to be participants in the working out of his redemptive plan, by completing "in [our] flesh ... what is lacking in

Christ's afflictions for the sake of his body, that is, the Church"
(Col 1:24). Thus, as members of Christ's Body, we don't bemoan
the reality of suffering in our lives or seek to flee every instance
of it, for we recognize that, if united with the Passion of Christ,
suffering can serve an important purpose in making us into the
people God intends us to be. To borrow again from Saint Paul,
"this slight momentary affliction is preparing for us an eternal
weight of glory beyond all comparison" (2 Cor 4:17).[41]

The fact that the Son of God became flesh and dwelt among
us, and that he took upon himself "untold sufferings" in order to
save us from our sins, casts a whole new light on our experiences
of pain and heartache. As Newman puts it, "The Gospel, which
has shed light in so many ways upon the state of this world, has
aided especially our view of *sufferings* to which human nature is
subjected; turning a punishment into a privilege, in the case of
all pain, and especially of bodily pain, which is the most mysterious of all."[42] How contrary this way of thinking is to the dom-
inant outlook in our culture! Even as Christians, blessed as we
are with the gift of revelation, we have to be intentional about
reminding ourselves of this truth. In a day and age when pain
medication is readily available, and with the modern amenities
that technology has made possible, it's incredibly easy to turn to
a quick fix at the first sign of personal discomfort. Though we
shouldn't necessarily feel guilty about taking aspirin or having
air conditioning, we should be on the lookout for occasions to
embrace some sort of momentary affliction as a form of self-denial in imitation of Christ, who was made "perfect through suffering" (Heb 2:10).

One of the most powerful biblical statements on redemptive
suffering comes from Saint Paul, who remarks that he rejoices
in his sufferings, which he sees as way of filling up in his own
flesh what is still lacking in Christ's afflictions (see Col 1:24,
which we've already had occasion to quote above). Without the
perspective that faith brings, suffering in this world would be
meaningless and a source only of grief and bitterness. But rec-

ognizing the role that it can play in our spiritual growth transforms suffering into something else entirely. Again, listen to the countercultural character of what Newman has to say about this topic: "And though [Paul] is speaking especially of persecution and other sufferings borne in the cause of the Gospel, yet it is our great privilege, as Scripture tells us, that all pain and trouble, borne in faith and patience, will be accounted as marks of Christ, grace-tokens from the absent Savior, and will be accepted and rewarded for His sake at the last day."[43] No suffering, however light — if it is offered up in union with the Passion of Christ — will go unnoticed on the last day. Even here and now, such suffering serves a grand purpose, for "suffering produces endurance, and endurance produces character, and character produces hope" (Rom 5:3–4). This is the purgative way in a nutshell.

SELF-DENIAL, THE TEST OF RELIGIOUS DEVOTION

The problem that often presents itself, however, is that we are not prepared to receive suffering as we should when it reaches us. That is to say, when we become sick or destitute or despised, we look at such occurrences only as unbearable trials and not as privileges. Even harboring the best of intentions, illness often distracts us from prayer, destitution produces crippling anxiety, and rejection causes feelings of loneliness. In such circumstances, it can be immensely difficult to maintain the disposition that we need in order for our sufferings to be meritorious. Barring some miraculous intervention by the Holy Spirit, the battle is lost if we wait to conjure up the right attitude in the midst of suffering. As with so many aspects of life, we have to prepare ourselves beforehand if want to avoid faltering when faced with a serious challenge.

Ordinarily, then, the foundation of the purgative process entails embracing such practices as fasting, almsgiving, and obedience to superiors. These are the sorts of disciplines that we can freely practice to prepare ourselves to suffer well when faced with trials over which we have no control. In this, as in so many other areas of the Christian life, the saints have charted the course for us:

> Who, on the other hand, does not at least perceive that all the glare and gaudiness of this world, its excitements, its keenly-pursued goods, its successes and its transports, its pomps and its luxuries, are not in character with that pale and solemn scene which faith must ever have in its eye? … So deeply have His Saints felt this, that when times were peaceful, and the Church was in safety, they could not rest in the lap of ease, and have secured to themselves hardnesses, lest the world should corrupt them.[44]

Due to our station in life, we may not be able to follow the example of a hermit such as Saint Anthony by fleeing to the desert. But we can imitate the general pattern set before us by the heroic ascetics of the Christian past in taking on forms of self-denial that are suited to the vocation to which God has called us.

The "daily self-denial" that Newman commends to us should begin at the very start of our day: "Let your very rising from your bed be a self-denial," he writes.[45] Rather than sleeping in or hitting the snooze button, we should work on getting out of bed immediately upon waking, which in itself requires a certain level of discipline. Then, as the day proceeds, the very rhythm of daily life will normally present all sorts of opportunities for practicing self-denial. "Let your meals be self-denials," Newman continues[46] — perhaps by eating smaller portions or by forgoing luxuries such as salt or sugar. Additionally, and this practice is sometimes the most difficult of all, "determine to yield to others in things indifferent, to go out of your way in small matters, to inconvenience yourself (so that no direct duty suffers by it), rather than [that] you should not meet with your daily discipline."[47] This type of self-denial can be accomplished in a number of ways, as, for instance, by yielding to another driver in traffic, by not returning an insult to a coworker, or by being patient when caring for an unruly child. In these and other ways, we gradually conform ourselves to the image of Christ, who "though he was in the form of God, did not count equality with God a thing to be grasped, but emptied himself, taking the form of a servant" (Phil 2:6–7). In fact, Newman goes so far as to describe self-denial as "the test of religious earnestness," by which he means we will know that we are truly devoted to God to the extent that we practice mortification in our daily lives.[48]

This being the case, one of the greatest dangers of our time is possessing what Newman calls "temporal advantages": i.e., wealth, prestige, comfort, and good health. Such temporal advantages, he notes, "have a strong tendency to render us self-confident," as we come to believe that we can provide for ourselves and are not reliant upon God.[49] If this tendency is not checked, it can very quickly transform into idolatry, wherein we elevate the temporal blessings of this life to the place where only God should properly reside. Given the seriousness of this danger, Newman reserves a strong warning against resting easy in comfortable affluence:

> If we have good health, and are in easy circumstances, let us beware of high-mindedness, self-sufficiency, self-conceit, arrogance; of delicacy of living, indulgences, luxuries, comforts. *Nothing is so likely to corrupt our hearts, and to seduce us from God, as to surround ourselves with comforts* — to have things our own way — to be the center of a sort of world, whether of things animate or inanimate, which minister to us. For then, in turn, we shall depend on them; they will become necessary to us; their very service and adulation will lead us to trust ourselves to them, and to idolize them.[50]

Stop for a moment and consider what Newman says in this excerpt. When we think about the things most likely to corrupt our hearts and draw us away from God, we normally have in mind grave sins, such as fornication or dishonest business dealings. But Newman suggests that the single likeliest source of corruption is surrounding ourselves with comforts!

Newman's thoughts on this topic have taken on even greater relevance since his death. We live in the most affluent civilization in human history, such that even the poorest members of our congregations are likely better off than 99 percent of those who have preceded us. The purgative way, then, absolutely demands that we develop a proper detachment from the temporal goods with which God has blessed us. This detachment, Newman cautions, cannot be in the mind only. It is very easy to convince ourselves that we are not *really* attached to our temporal goods, but it is by practicing almsgiving and fasting and simplicity that we prove it. Given the seductive manner in which our society tempts us to make idols of our possessions, let us heed Newman's warnings on this subject. In a footnote appended to his sermon on bodily suffering, Newman provides a quote that puts this issue in sharp relief: "It is a most miserable state for a man to have everything according to his desire, and quietly to enjoy the pleasures of life. There needs no more to expose him to eternal misery."[51] If providence itself does not deprive us of the pleasures of life, then we must have the wherewithal, in cooperation with God's grace, to practice self-denial in such a way that we come to trust in God alone.

EXCURSUS: THE DANGER OF RICHES
While basic material comforts can slowly deaden our sensitivity to the things of God, accumulating a substantial amount of wealth is to place oneself in a particularly perilous situation. In one of his bluntest sermons on this topic ("The Danger of Riches"), Newman notes that this is one area where many Christians tend to overlook the seriousness with which Scripture

approaches the matter. In society, he says, there are religious persons who are able to conquer all sorts of sinful desires, including lust, gluttony, drunkenness, and love of amusements. But, when it comes to wealth, "they cannot easily rid themselves of a secret feeling that it gives them a footing to stand upon, an importance, a superiority."[52] Like the rich young ruler mentioned in the Gospels, many of us are willing to follow God up to a certain point but balk at the notion that this commitment should impinge upon our financial well-being. "To risk all upon Christ's word seems somehow unnatural to [us]," Newman writes. So we "are content to remain as [we] are, and do not contemplate a change."[53]

As a justification for our half-heartedness, we are tempted to make a distinction between *having* money and *loving* money. In Newman's words: "It is usual to dismiss such passages [i.e., those that highlight the dangers of wealth] with the remark that they are directed, not against those who have, but against those who trust in, riches."[54] Newman is suspicious of this distinction for a couple of reasons. First, he notes that in many instances the words of Scripture accent the *possessing* without including any qualifications about "trusting in." So, for example: "But woe to you that are rich, for you have received your consolation" (Lk 6:24). In this case, the consolation of possessing wealth is directly contrasted with "the comfort which is promised to the Christian in the list of Beatitudes."[55] Or, consider Luke 18:25, where Our Lord bluntly states that "it is easier for a camel to go through the eye of a needle than for a rich man to enter the kingdom of God." In these passages and others, the warning falls squarely on being rich and stops there.

Lest his listeners miss the point, Newman goes a step further: "In truth, that our Lord meant to speak of riches as being in some sense a calamity to the Christian, is plain, not only from such texts as the foregoing, but from His praises and recommendation on the other hand of poverty."[56] Thus, Jesus instructs his disciples, "Sell your possessions, and give alms; provide yourselves with purses that do not grow old" (Lk 12:33). Similarly, when hosting a celebration, do not call on your friends or your wealthy neighbors, Jesus teaches, but "invite the poor, the maimed, the lame, the blind, and you will be blessed, because they cannot repay you. You will be repaid at the resurrection of the just" (Lk 14:13–14). In like manner, Saint James writes: "Has not God chosen the poor in the world to be rich in faith and heirs of the kingdom which he has promised to those who love him?" (Jas 2:5).[57] In all of these ways, Scripture holds up for our consideration the blessedness of the poor.[58]

Why is merely having wealth so dangerous? For Newman, the danger is that "[worldly possessions] are present; God is unseen. They are means at hand of effecting what we want."[59] By their very nature, wealth and possessions easily become idols to us. Ironically, we can read about the Israelites bowing before a golden calf and can scoff at their foolishness without ever realizing that very often, in our day-to-day lives, we relate to money in precisely the same manner. As Newman summarizes the matter, worldly possessions "promise and are able to be gods to us, and such gods too as require no service, but, like dumb idols, exalt the worshipper, impressing him with a notion of his own power and security."[60] Think about it: Money is an inanimate object that provides us with a sense of power, falsely leading us to believe that we can secure our well-being if only we have enough of it. Furthermore, unlike God, money (seemingly) makes no demands of us. We can reap the benefits of having wealth without its ever making harsh demands upon how we live our lives. Could there be a more apt description of an idol?

When we reach the point of thinking that our wealth can provide us with security, we have lost sight of the true end of human existence: namely, to serve God in this world and to be happy with him forever in heaven.[61] In place of this truth, we substitute a lie, deceiving ourselves into believing that money can provide the security that is available only by trusting in God. Christ left us a powerful warning against this line of thinking.

In Luke, chapter 12, Jesus tells the parable of a certain rich man who planned to tear down his barns and build larger ones so that he could store the surplus grain from his harvest. When making these plans, the man thought, "I'll say to myself, 'You have plenty of grain laid up for many years. Take life easy; eat, drink, and be merry.' But God said to him, 'You fool! This very night your life will be demanded from you' " (vv. 19–20, NIV). None of us knows the day or hour when we will be ushered into God's presence. At that moment, our 401(k)s and stock portfolios will do nothing for us. All that will matter is what we have done for the "least of these" (see Mt 25:31–46).

"The danger," then, "of *possessing* riches is the carnal security to which they lead; that of '*desiring*' and *pursuing* them, is, that an object of this world is thus set before us as the aim and end of life."[62] Making an object our primary pursuit in life is, as we have seen, the very definition of idolatry. And ironically, riches fail to provide even the temporal goods they promise to deliver. As Newman observes, "Nor is it a slight aggravation of the evil, that anxiety is almost sure to attend [gain]. A life of money-getting is a life of care; from the first there is a fearful anticipation of loss in various ways to depress and unsettle the mind; nay to haunt it, till a man finds he can think about nothing else."[63] In stark contrast to the anxiety that nags at those keen on preserving their wealth, Sacred Scripture promises "a peace that surpasses all understanding" to Christ's followers (Phil 4:7, NIV). This promise is guaranteed by Christ himself, who taught that God the Father knows our material needs and will provide for them (Mt 6:8). "Look at the birds of the air: they neither sow nor reap nor gather into barns, and yet [our] heavenly Father feeds them" (Mt 6:26). Are we not more valuable than the birds of the air? "There is no excuse then for that absorbing pursuit of wealth," Newman concludes, for Christ "has expressly told us that the [necessities] of life shall never fail His faithful follower."[64]

A parish priest once explained it to me this way: If we knew we were going to die this evening, would we be sad to leave behind the possessions that we have accumulated? In a certain sense, the more we have, the more difficult it is to think about letting it go in order to be with God. The stark truth of the matter is this, though: we came forth from our mothers' wombs with nothing, and we will depart this life with nothing (see Job 1:21). In the end, the only thing that matters is what we do with the time in between on behalf of the kingdom of God. Viewed from the perspective of eternity, possessions are like weights that drag us back down to the earth when we should be longing to be united with God in heaven. If we want to prepare for a good death, one of the most concrete steps we can take is to divest ourselves as much as possible of our surplus wealth. From a Catholic perspective, our attachment to earthly goods is one of the things that, for many of us, the fires of purgatory will have to burn away.

Now, all of the above being true — and I want to be careful not to say anything that would slacken the force of Christ's commands — Catholic moral theology has traditionally stressed that the life of charity must never be lived out in such a way that it violates the demands of justice. So, for example, a father has a responsibility to provide for his family. If a father were to give away all that he had, such that he was no longer able to clothe and feed his children, he would be acting unjustly and, thus, we could rightly conclude that he had misunderstood what the call of Christ demanded of him.[65] The danger here, and it is a serious one, is that it's exceedingly easy to move from the thought of providing for our families to a frame of mind in which we are deceiving ourselves about what that provision requires.[66] Because mothers and fathers bear the responsibility of caring for their offspring, perhaps we face the temptation of greed more intensely than those who are celibate. Whatever our state in life, we should not be deceived: "No servant can serve two masters; for either he will hate the one and love the other, or he will be devoted to the one and despise the other. You cannot serve God and mammon" (Lk 16:13). Newman is one of the strongest prophetic voices of the modern period who reinforces this charge from the Gospel. The dutiful Christian will be careful to heed his (and the Gospels') warnings.[67]

STAGE TWO: THE ILLUMINATIVE WAY

For the Christian, self-denial is not an end in itself, of course, but is always directed toward the knowledge and love of God. Thus, the purgative way, if it is supplemented by worship and study of the Faith, will naturally flower into the second stage of the spiritual life, which the saints call the *illuminative* way. As we free ourselves from sinful desires and disordered attachments, our knowledge of God will correspondingly increase, on the condition that we abide in Christ by rooting our existence in the liturgy and faith of the Church. That latter point, about the liturgy, is a significant one. Discussions of the worshipping life of the Church can be found threaded throughout Newman's preaching, because, for him, worship is the primary means by which we encounter, and thus come to know, the living God.

From Newman's perspective, we misunderstand what it means to know God if we approach this knowing in the same way that we think about knowledge gained through scientific research or the study of history. In short, God is not an *object* for study, as if we could somehow know God by memorizing a list of facts about him. Rather, God is a loving communion of Persons — Father, Son, and Holy Spirit — whom we can truly know only through a mutual exchange of love; that is, by entering into a covenant relationship with him. Newman describes these two ways of knowing as *notional apprehension*, which refers to "grasping an idea," and *real assent*, that is, "deciding to respond to a reality."[68] Though notional apprehension of ideas has its place, saving faith necessarily involves real assent, which in religious matters means entrusting the entirety of one's life to the divine will. Coming to know God is far more like entering into a marital covenant than like studying for an exam. Knowing God requires that we put our very selves on the line. It involves both commitment and sacrifice.

For a biblical analogy, we can think of the account of Jacob wrestling with the Lord on the bank of the river Jabbok (Gn 32). On the night before he is scheduled to reunite with his brother Esau, Jacob gets locked in a marathon struggle with a mysterious, unnamed figure, whom the passage later describes as a manifestation of the divine presence. As daybreak approaches, Jacob's opponent realizes that he will not be able to overpower him, so he asks Jacob to release him. Jacob says that he will do so only if the figure agrees to bless him in return. The Lord does bless him and also gives him a new name, Israel. Henceforth Jacob will no longer be known as "trickster" or "con man," but as the one who struggled with God and overcame. Tellingly, Jacob leaves the encounter blessed but also wounded, and he limps for the rest of his life on account of this encounter with God. Read allegorically, this narrative is a parable of our own spiritual journey. To know God — to really know him — is to struggle with the callings that God has placed upon our lives. The blessings that accompany these callings are immeasurable, but they come at a cost. As in the case of Jacob, blessing and woundedness are inextricably intertwined. Today, the Church reminds us of this reality by marking those who are being baptized with the Sign of the Cross. Baptism, then, is not a sentimental ceremony meant to warm our hearts but involves placing a person's entire life under the Sign of the Cross, so that God's claim upon that person takes precedence over all other concerns.

To turn away from God because of the difficulties and self-sacrifice involved, however, would be to miss out on true, lasting happiness, for "God alone is the happiness of our souls."[69] "We may indeed love [created things] with great intenseness," Newman notes, "but such affection, when disjoined from the love of the Creator, is like a stream running in a narrow channel, impetuous, vehement, turbid."[70] The desires of our heart cannot be constrained within the confines of earthly experiences. The heart, as it were, expands outward, seeking a reality that is proportional to its energies. As Newman puts it:

> Created natures cannot open us, or elicit the ten thousand mental senses which belong to us, and through which we really live. None but the presence of our Maker can enter us; for to none besides can the whole heart in all its thoughts and feelings be unlocked and subjected. "Behold," He says, "I stand at the door and knock; if any man hear My voice and open the door, I will come in to him, and will sup with him, and he with Me" [Rev 3:20]. ... It is this feeling of simple and absolute confidence and communion, which soothes and satisfies those to whom it is vouchsafed.[71]

Friendship with God, in the language of Newman, is "the stay of the soul." If we try to ground our happiness in anything other than God, we will, in effect, create a self-imposed prison for our hearts. As Newman says, "We need to escape from ourselves to something beyond; and much as we may wish it otherwise, and may try to make idols to ourselves, nothing short of God's presence is our true refuge."[72] The One "who is infinite can alone be [the heart's] measure," for "He alone can answer to the mysterious assemblage of feelings and thoughts which it has within it."[73]

Thankfully, God has not left us alone in the world, reliant on our own capacities in order to know him, but is constantly reaching out to sinners in diverse ways. The liturgy, Newman says, is the privileged means by which we come to know God, for at Mass we hear the voice of God speaking to us (through the proclamation of Sacred Scripture) and receive God's grace into our hearts (in holy Communion). Even as an Anglican, before accepting the fullness of Catholic sacramental theology, Newman had a very high view of the role that the sacraments play

in our coming to know God. For instance, in a sermon titled
"Worship, a Preparation for Christ's Coming," Newman presents prayer, both private and communal, as a way of preparing to
meet God at the moment of death. He then goes on to say:

> And what is true of the ordinary services of reli-
> gion, public and private, holds in a still higher or
> rather in a special way, as regards the sacramental
> ordinances of the Church. In these is manifested
> in greater or less degree, according to the mea-
> sure of each, that Incarnate Savior, who is one day
> to be our Judge, and who is enabling us to bear
> His presence then, by imparting it to us in mea-
> sure now. A thick black veil is spread between this
> world and the next. ... In the Gospel this veil is
> not removed; it remains, but every now and then
> marvelous disclosures are made to us of what is
> behind it. At times we seem to catch a glimpse of
> a Form which we shall hereafter see face to face.
> We approach, and in spite of the darkness, our
> hands, or our head, or our brow, or our lips be-
> come, as it were, sensible of the contact of some-
> thing more than earthly.[74]

In this world of sense, we see through a glass darkly (see 1
Cor 13:12). It is as if a veil, or a curtain, stands between us and
God. For as long as we are alive, that veil is never completely lifted, but in the liturgy, Newman suggests, we are given a glimpse
behind it. Through the sacraments, all baptized Christians are
initiated into the mysticism that we sometimes assume is re-
served for the saints. The celebration of the sacraments, then,
cannot be reduced to a matter of symbolic ritual, for on these
occasions we come into direct contact with the person of Christ.
Via these privileged encounters, Our Lord prepares us to meet
him in glory:

We know not where we are, but we have been bathing in water, and a voice tells us that it is blood.
Or we have a mark signed upon our foreheads,
and it spake of Calvary. Or we recollect a hand
laid upon our heads, and surely it had the print
of nails in it, and resembled His who with a touch
gave sight to the blind and raised the dead. Or we
have been eating and drinking; and it was not a
dream surely, that One fed us from His wounded side, and renewed our nature by the heavenly meat He gave. Thus in many ways He, who is
Judge to us, prepares us to be judged — He, who
is to glorify us, prepares us to be glorified, that
He may not take us unawares; but that when the
voice of the Archangel sounds, and we are called
to meet the Bridegroom, we may be ready.[75]

This is what it looks like to attain real knowledge of God.
When we have the mark of the cross signed upon our foreheads,
it is Christ making that sign. When the words of absolution are
spoken over us, it is God's voice that we are hearing. When we
receive holy Communion, it is none other than our Risen Lord,
who feeds us with his Body and Blood.

STAGE THREE: THE UNITIVE WAY

In light of these truths, Newman suggests that if we want to
gauge our preparedness for heaven, we should begin by exam-
ining the state of our hearts and minds while at church. We
sometimes mistakenly envision heaven as an extension and
intensification of our favorite earthly pleasures, perhaps something like a backyard barbecue in the sky. But heaven, Newman points out, "is not like this world"; it "is much more like
— *a church*."[76] Since heaven will involve the eternal contemplation and adoration of God, the nearest approximation we have
to this experience on earth is the liturgy. "We hear nothing,"

Newman says, "of [worldly interests] in a church." Rather, "here we hear solely and entirely of *God*. We praise Him, worship Him, sing to Him, thank Him, confess to Him, give ourselves up to Him, and ask His blessing."[77] If we find ourselves consistently bored or distracted at Mass, we may want to reevaluate our standing before God, because how we experience worship now is, in effect, a barometer of our preparedness for heaven. "A careless, a sensual, an unbelieving mind, a mind destitute of the love and fear of God … would feel as little pleasure, [on] the last day, at the words, 'Enter into the joy of thy Lord,' as it does now at the words, 'Let us pray.' Nay, much less, because, while we are in a church, we may turn our thoughts to other subjects, and contrive to forget that God is looking on us; but that will not be possible in heaven."[78]

The positive side of this whole discussion, however, is that when we are properly prepared, ultimate happiness is made available to us. Whereas "heaven would be hell to an irreligious man," to those who have been sanctified it will be bliss unimaginable — far exceeding the joy of any earthly experience.[79] As Saint Paul testifies, "What no eye has seen, nor ear heard, nor the heart of man conceived, what God has prepared for those who love him" (1 Cor 2:9, NIV, slightly revised). When the veil is finally lifted, "we shall see [God] face to face." Now we "know in part; then [we] shall know fully, even as [we are] fully known" (1 Cor 13:12, NIV). There are few better descriptions of the unitive way than what Saint Paul provides here, and as Newman shows us, the liturgy is the privileged means by which God grants us a glimpse of what awaits us in eternity. In each celebration of the Mass, we are provided a foretaste of that blessedness that we will know fully in heaven.

Furthermore, the Mass is a regular reminder that we do not journey to God alone. Whenever we recite the Apostles' Creed, we confess that we believe in the communion of saints, and the very structure of the liturgy affirms that truth. The preface, for instance, reminds us that in singing the Sanctus — "Holy, holy,

holy, Lord God of Hosts … " — we join our voices with all of the angels and archangels in proclaiming God's glory. This liturgical theology is entirely biblical, rooted in the book of Revelation's vision of how worship on earth is intimately united with the endless praise offered by the martyrs and the angels before the throne of God. This reality of our communion with the saints in heaven should encourage us not to lose heart. As the author of Hebrews urges, "Therefore, since we are surrounded by so great a cloud of witnesses, let us also lay aside every weight, and sin which clings so closely, and let us run with perseverance the race that is set before us, looking to Jesus the pioneer and perfecter of our faith. … Consider him who endured from sinners such hostility against himself, so that you may not grow weary or fainthearted" (Heb 12:1–3). I am not a runner, but I've heard from good friends who participate in marathons that there are few encouragements more motivating than to run by supporters who are cheering you on (particularly if those supporters have Gatorade in hand). Happily, we have this same kind of support in the spiritual life, surrounded as we are by a great cloud of witnesses.

This imagery of running a race shows up a few times in the New Testament, and it presents a helpful lens through which to view Newman's spirituality. As we have seen, Newman can be quite demanding in the regimen that he proposes for achieving spiritual growth. All that he has to say on these matters, however, is meant to prepare us to compete successfully in the race that God has marked out for us. In this light, any practices of self-denial that we adopt are not ends in themselves. Rather, they are always oriented toward union with God. The goal is to reach the finish line, not to be ascetical for asceticism's sake.

And through it all, Newman insists, we are energized and sustained by God's grace, which Newman describes as a "sovereign, energetic power" capable of elevating our nature to a supernatural end.[80] One of the ways God's grace empowers us to run with perseverance is by freeing us from the burden of our sins.

Consonant with the admonition in the Letter to the Hebrews to look to Jesus, Saint Paul stresses that we cannot run successfully if we are fixated on our past. Paul's strategy is one that we all should adopt: "Forgetting what lies behind and straining forward to what lies ahead, I press on toward the goal for the prize of the upward call of God in Christ Jesus" (Phil 3:13–14). In the battleground of the spiritual life, one of Satan's preferred tactics is to remind us of our history, seeking to convince us that our sins make us unworthy to be called children of God. That is why Paul urges us to forget what lies behind and, instead, to focus on the faithfulness of God. To paraphrase Romans 3:4: though every person be found a liar, God will remain true. In other words, God would not call us to this race if he did not also intend to grant us the means of finishing it. For ourselves:

> Let us follow the Saints, as they follow Christ; so that, when He comes in judgment, and the wretched world sinks to perdition, "on us sinners, His servants, hoping in the multitude of His mercies, He may vouchsafe to bestow some portion and fellowship with His Holy Apostles and Martyrs, with John, Stephen, Matthias, Barnabas, Ignatius, Alexander, Marcelline, Peter, Felicity, Perpetua, Agatha, Lucy, Agnes, Cicely, Anastasia, and all His Saints, not for the value of our merit, but according to the bounty of His pardon, through the same Christ our Lord."[81]

If we faithfully run the race set before us, what awaits us at the finish line is a reality far exceeding anything we can presently imagine. Newman paints a picture of this reality by talking about the contrast between the visible world and the invisible one — "the world we see, and the world we do not see."[82] The world of sense is more immediate to us; therefore, we are unlikely to doubt its existence. As Newman says, "We have but to lift up our eyes and look around us, and we have proof of it."[83] Nevertheless, the hustle and bustle of this visible realm "does not interfere with the existence of that other world," which is more real, because it is where God dwells.[84]

We daily "hold communion" with this "world of spirits," Newman continues, even if we don't consciously recognize it.[85] By a special grace, some among us are able to develop a sharper sense for seeing the reality that lies behind the sensible world. Newman urges us to seek this gift — to ask God for the capacity to see the world in all its fullness, as opposed to settling on the truncated image of a purely physical reality. As a word of encouragement, Newman highlights elements of nature that testify to God's life-giving power. Consider, for instance, the season of spring, when "there is a sudden rush and burst outwardly of that hidden life which God has lodged in the material world."[86] On one level, this bursting forth of new life seems so natural to us, principally because we witness it annually. If we take a step back, however, and try to see it again for the first time, we might be struck by how awe-inspiring the whole process is: "Who would think, except from his experience of former springs all through his life, who could conceive two or three months before, that it was possible that the face of nature, which then seemed so lifeless, should become so splendid and varied?"[87] The dying and rising to life that we witness annually in the transition from winter to spring, Newman proposes, is a presaging of the future renewal of the entire creation, in which the dead in Christ will be raised to eternal glory (cf. Rv 21).

When we consider the unitive way, therefore, we ought to stir up a "longing after that which we do not see."[88] For if we could see now even a glimpse of the destiny that awaits us in the beatific vision, we would be freed from our disordered attachment to the things of this world — things that are good in themselves, yes, but not ultimately satisfying. Those who are able to foster this holy detachment, Newman concludes, are truly blessed:

> O blessed they indeed, who are destined for the
> sight of those wonders in which they now stand,
> at which they now look, but which they do not
> recognize! Blessed they who shall at length be-
> hold what as yet mortal eye hath not seen, and
> faith only enjoys! ... The life then begun, we
> know, will last forever; yet surely if memory be
> to us then what it is now, that will be a day much
> to be observed unto the Lord through all the
> ages of eternity. We may increase indeed forever
> in knowledge and in love, still that first waking
> from the dead, the day at once of our birth and
> our espousals, will ever be endeared and hallowed
> in our thoughts. ... Earthly words are indeed all
> worthless to minister to such high anticipations.
> Let us close our eyes and keep silence.[89]

Finally, while we live in expectation of the full outworking of God's salvific plan, we ought not to think of the unitive aspect as merely a future reality. When Jesus explained the reason for the Incarnation, he told his followers, "I came that they [i.e., the redeemed] may have life, and have it abundantly" (Jn 10:10). This abundant life is available to us now — most intensely in our partaking of the divine nature through the reception of Christ's Body and Blood, but also, outside of Mass, whenever we stop to direct our attention to the unseen world. "Though thou art in a body of flesh, a member of this world," Newman writes, "thou hast but to kneel down reverently in prayer, and thou art at once in the society of Saints and Angels."[90] Let us do all that we can to stir up a livelier sense of our communion with those beings who already find themselves before the heavenly throne, asking that by God's grace we might soon join their company in the eternal contemplation of Our Lord's indescribable presence.

3

LEARNING THE NEW LANGUAGE OF CHRIST

In his poetic masterpiece the *Purgatorio*, Dante allegorically portrays the journey to God as a long, arduous trek up a steep mountain. Anyone who has made the effort to be freed from sin can identify with Dante's imagery. The process of coming to know and love God involves a great deal of joy, but it is not easy. Even a missionary as zealous as Saint Paul testified, "I do not run aimlessly, I do not box as one beating the air; but I pommel my body and subdue it, lest after preaching to others I myself should be disqualified" (1 Cor 9:26–27). This contest that we are in clearly demands a great deal of sacrifice and self-discipline.

Newman uses a range of metaphors to communicate the same idea. At one point in his sermons, for instance, he compares the process of sanctification to language acquisition: "It is not an easy thing," he remarks, "to learn that new language which Christ has brought us."[91] Anyone who has attempted to learn a second language knows precisely what Newman is getting at here. Mastering a new language requires time and effort. Realistically, the best way of going about it is to immerse oneself totally in a different culture. Regardless of which strategy one adopts, it's clear that this goal cannot be tackled haphazardly or lackadaisically. Learning a new language requires both intentionality and discipline, and only the truly dedicated will succeed.

Like Newman, Saint Thomas Aquinas recognized the challenges inherent in pursuing holiness. Prior to times of study, Aquinas would pray for deliverance from "the twofold darkness into which I was born — sin and ignorance."[92] This prayer draws our attention to the effects of original sin. Whereas our first parents "walked with God" in the garden (Gn 3:8), we no longer enjoy this level of intimacy with our Creator. Original sin has wounded both the human will and the human mind, such that we don't automatically or easily draw near to God. Even those who have been baptized continue to live under the burden of concupiscence, our inclination toward sinful desires.

In light of sin's baleful effects, it's imperative that we practice "rigorous self-denial."[93] From Newman's vantage point, the one who says that he loves Christ but does not practice self-denial is almost certainly deceiving himself. "Rigorous self-denial," he writes, is not simply "a chief duty" but "may be considered *the* test whether we are Christ's disciples" or not.[94] Admittedly, upon hearing these points, some might worry that Newman is reducing the pursuit of holiness to a matter of human effort. But what he says here closely aligns with the biblical vision of discipleship. Jesus, for example, instructs his followers to take up their crosses daily (Lk 9:23). Other parts of the New Testament talk about disciplining our bodies (1 Cor 9:27), about toiling and striving (1 Tm 4:10), and about running with endurance the race that has been marked out for us (Heb 12:1). It is true that apart from God's grace we can do nothing, but that does not mean we are passive recipients of that grace. In line with the scriptural vision of discipleship, we are called to cooperate with the grace that God extends to us.

A Religion of Practice, Not Sentiment

As you might expect by this point, Newman does not present a vague or partial picture of discipleship, leaving the reader to fill in the details. Rather, he gives clear indications of what the *kenotic*, or self-emptying, life should look like. Four main points stand out. First, the way of self-denial that Christ calls us to demands singularity of purpose. In one of his sermons on obedience, Newman notes that far too many Christians "go on with a double aim, trying to serve both God and mammon."[95] Like the rich young ruler spoken of in Matthew 19, we may have some level of desire to follow Jesus but then turn away sad when we realize that Christ is calling us to divest ourselves of possessions or prestige. Newman remarks that those who have this mindset obey God only when they are able to do so "without offending the bad Master that rules them."[96] But as Our Lord warns us elsewhere in the Gospels, "no one can serve two masters. ... You cannot serve [both] God and mammon" (Mt 6:24). This insight holds true for whatever thing we may be tempted to elevate above God — whether wealth, prestige, pleasure, or some other finite good. Given the human propensity for idolatry, we need to plead with God to grant us the grace of an undivided heart.

Second, at the heart of discipleship is faithfulness in the ordinary duties of life. In the same sermon on obedience, Newman observes that "God does great things by plain methods."[97] We sometimes buck against doing plain things, however, precisely "*because* they are plain."[98] As an illustration of this tendency, Newman points to the Old Testament figure Naaman, a military commander from Syria who suffers from leprosy. When Naaman learns that the prophet Elisha might have the power to heal him, he travels to Israel to seek Elisha's help. Upon learning that a foreign officer is coming to meet him, the prophet sends a messenger to say to Naaman, "Go and wash in the Jordan seven times, and your flesh shall be restored, and you shall be clean" (2 Kgs 5:10). Scripture tells us that Naaman is angry when he receives these instructions, because he assumed that Elisha would personally meet with him and heal him on the spot. Eventually, the servants of Naaman convince their master to heed Elisha's directive, saying, "My father, if the prophet had commanded you to do some great thing, would you not have done it? How much rather, then, when he says to you, 'Wash, and be clean'?" (2 Kgs 5:13). Not surprisingly, after Naaman follows the prophet's instructions, he is healed from his malady.

Though it's unlikely that we will ever receive a prophetic command to bathe in a river seven times, there is an important lesson to take away from God's dealings with Naaman. On occasion, we mistakenly assume that following Christ must have a dramatic element in order to be worth our time. In other words, we imagine ourselves making great sacrifices or accomplishing heroic deeds, when, in fact, the means of our being made holy lie right in front of us, in the ordinary responsibilities that are required by our station in life. Newman knew that many Christians suffer from the temptation of neglecting plain things, so when he gave advice regarding self-denial, he normally kept his admonitions realistic and concrete. For example:

> Avoid society which is likely to mislead you; flee from the very shadow of evil; you cannot be too careful; better be a little too strict than a little too easy — it is the safer side. Abstain from reading books which are dangerous to you. Turn from bad thoughts when they arise, set about some business, begin conversing with some friend, or say to yourself the Lord's Prayer reverently. When[ever] you are urged by temptation ... shut your eyes and think of Christ's precious blood-shedding.[99]

The counsel that Newman gives here (and in other sermons) is all very straightforward and quotidian. For him, the life of discipleship that Christ calls us to must be lived out daily and in the smallest of matters. Rather than aiming to accomplish something great, we ought to recognize that "the self-denial which is pleasing to Christ consists in little things."[100] "Consistency," not performing miraculous feats, is "the mark of a saint,"[101] and as we show our faithfulness in little areas, God will entrust us with more.

As is obvious from the above, "there is nothing sentimental about Newman's spirituality."[102] That is to say, Newman gets down to brass tacks when discussing the life of discipleship. One of the central points of advice that he gives in his sermons is for Christians to talk less and do more (it doesn't get much more straightforward than that!). Clearly, Newman was not totally averse to discussing spiritual matters: his written works could fill several bookshelves. But he also recognized that, for far too many Christians, feeling religious and talking about religion often stand in the place of actual obedience.[103] In light of this tendency, Newman consistently pressed his flock to focus on habitual obedience, particularly with respect to small matters. In his estimation,

> [the one] who does one little deed of obedience, whether [denying] himself some comfort to relieve the sick and needy, or curb[ing] his temper, or forgiv[ing] an enemy ... evinces more true faith than could be shown by the most fluent religious conversation, [or] the most intimate knowledge of Scripture doctrine. ... Yet how many are there who sit still with folded hands, dreaming, doing nothing at all, thinking they have done everything, or need do nothing, when they merely have had these good *thoughts*, which will save no one![104]

In another sermon, Newman provides a litany of the kinds of actions that lead to true holiness: "give alms ... shut your ears to praise ... curb your tongue, and turn away your eyes ... be up at prayer 'a great while before the day.' "[105] There is nothing particularly heroic about these sacrifices, but that is where their power lies. Our faithfulness in small matters is precisely what lays the groundwork for us to face severe trials. For whoever "is faithful in a very little [will be] faithful also in much" (Lk 16:10).

Third, Newman reminds us that life in Christ is a marathon, not a sprint. "To take up the cross," he remarks, "is not a great action done once for all."[106] Rather, it takes a lifetime of humble, regular obedience in order to attain complete conformity to the person of Christ. Just as with physical exercise, we can throw ourselves off course by taking on too much too quickly. Because we live in a culture that prizes instant gratification, we might like to skip straight from small acts of self-denial to mystical visions and performing miracles, the kinds of activities we associate with great saints. But this outlook is mistaken. As Newman straightforwardly advises, "Begin not *with* the end[, but] begin with the beginning; mount[ing] up the heavenly ladder step by step."[107] God's grace, Newman adds, will increase according to our need. For God has established it as a rule of providence "that those who act up to their light, shall be rewarded with clearer light."[108]

Finally, and this point is vital, the life we live in Christ — however much it involves self-denial — ought also to be characterized by joy. In the pantheon of great spiritual writers, Newman was one who emphasized what might be called the harsher side of the Gospel. We've seen this facet of his thought already in the strictness of his moral guidelines. In contrast to "the religion of the day," which sought to explain away divine wrath, Newman was intent on communicating the more difficult parts of the Gospel.[109] But none of this means for a moment that Christians have an excuse to lack joy. "Gloom is no Christian temper," Newman insists, and "that repentance is not real, which has not love in it."[110] Even our "self-chastisement" should be "sweetened by faith and cheerfulness."[111] The inspiration for these thoughts came to Newman from Saint Paul, who, even though he experienced great trials — e.g., arrest, imprisonment, beatings, shipwreck — testified that he had learned to be content in all things (Phil 4:11–12). Keeping Paul's experience in mind, we can see clearly that joy cannot be equated simply with superficial feelings of happiness. The New Testament vision is much richer than that. So is Newman's. When he writes that "we must live in sunshine, even when we sorrow," he's not simply suggesting that we put on a happy face.[112] He's reminding us that we live perpetually in God's presence and challenging us to allow supernatural love and peace to radiate through us. A life of self-denial that is devoid of joy is stoicism, not Christianity. Therefore, "let us seek the grace of a cheerful heart, an even temper, sweetness, gentleness, and brightness of mind, as walking in [God's] light, and by His grace."[113]

BECOME A SAINT: WHAT ELSE IS THERE?

A shorthand way of referring to the way of life described above is to say that we are all called to be saints. The purpose of life is not to accumulate wealth or make a name for oneself, but to be filled completely with the love of God. Simply stated, a saint is one who has become so filled with the Holy Spirit that all of that person's desires and energies are oriented toward fulfilling the will of God. If becoming a saint is the overarching purpose of human existence, one of the first steps each of us needs to take is to dispel the thought that this way of life is impossible *for me*. We can fall into the trap of admiring the lives of saints while assuming that we ourselves are just not wired like them. This outlook has even seeped into colloquial ways of speaking: "It's only human nature," we say. Or, "Boys will be boys." Though phrases of this sort may not be ill-intentioned, they can, each in its own way, gloss over actions that are objectively sinful.

Newman points out that this mindset is precisely how worldly persons think: "Men of this world, carnal men, unbelieving men, do not believe that the temptations which they themselves experience and to which they yield, can be overcome."[114] Those who walk through life apart from God's grace assume that it's simply not possible to avoid sinning. Rather than seeking the grace to overcome sin, "they reason themselves into the notion that to sin is their very nature, and, therefore, is no fault of theirs."[115] Newman is right, I think, when he concludes that this way of thinking is effectively to deny the very existence of sin. If this or that vice is truly attributable to my nature, then I have nothing to feel guilty about. Sinning, from this perspective, is no different from sneezing, so to dwell on my fault is only to encourage a kind of neurosis.

When worldly minded persons read about the lives of the saints, Newman goes on to say, "they conclude either that these have not had the [same] temptations which they [themselves experience] … or that [the Saints never] overcame them."[116] In other words, carnal persons look at the saints and assume either that they were hypocrites — who practiced in private the sins they denounced in public — or that they never experienced the full weight of temptation that the rest of us do. What is not possible, according to this mindset, is that there have been real-life individuals who were tempted in every way, like the rest of us, yet who attained victory over that temptation.

Newman calls this way of looking at the world a "false and narrow" view.[117] Ironically, those who adopt this misguided view assume that they know the world and understand human nature more deeply than poor Christians do. But what they fail to see — or, perhaps, refuse to see — is human nature as it exists under the operation of grace. In other words, they assume that human nature, in its natural capacities, is the highest bar that humans can attain. They know nothing, then, of what Newman calls "the second nature," which is a supernatural gift — namely, the influence of "the Almighty Spirit upon our first and fallen nature."[118] As Newman so wonderfully puts it, the saints' "actions are as beautiful as fiction, yet as real as fact."[119] In their lives, grace has elevated nature to attain supernatural ends. The overcoming of mortal sin is indeed the destiny of all who shall be saved, but we celebrate in a particular way the lives of the saints, Newman points out, because they conquered sin "with a determination and a vigor, a promptitude and a success, beyond anyone else."[120] Their lives put to rest the notion that any one of us has to spend another day enslaved to sin.

In our day and age, this contrast between the way that worldly persons think and the way that the saints think is arguably most evident in the realm of sexual morality. Looking at Hollywood films and popular advertisements, one could easily conclude that chastity is not only impossible but also unnatural. According to the predominant cultural outlook, if a person is not actively pursuing sexual gratification, he or she is missing out on what makes life most enjoyable, even meaningful. Entire films (e.g., *40 Days and 40 Nights*) are premised on the supposed insanity of abstaining from sexual activity, and mocking virgins is a standard gag on television shows and in movies. Within our hypersexualized culture, love is reduced to erotic expression and human beings are viewed as being basically no different from our mammalian counterparts.

Newman will have none of it. As an experienced pastor and counselor of souls, he, of course, recognizes the struggle that being chaste involves. Concupiscence continues to weigh down even those who have been regenerated in baptism. But to move from that observation to denying that temptation can be overcome is to empty the cross of its power. God's grace is effectual to elevate our human nature beyond what we at first assume possible. We know this to be the case, because we have witnessed it in the lives of the saints — preeminently in the life of the Blessed Virgin Mary, whose entire existence was characterized by obedience to God's will. The shining example of Mary shatters the lie of the Devil that sin is our fate, and thus, we are wise to run to her whenever temptation weighs heavily upon us. By opening ourselves up to grace in this way, we give powerful witness to the truth of the Catholic Faith. As Newman says:

> It is the boast of the Catholic Religion, that it has the gift of making the young heart chaste; and why is this, but that it gives us Jesus Christ for our food, and Mary for our nursing Mother? Fulfil this boast in yourselves; prove to the world that you are following no false teaching, vindicate the glory of your Mother Mary, whom the world blasphemes, in the very face of the world, by the simplicity of your deportment, and the sanctity of your words and deeds. Go to her for the royal heart of innocence. She is the beautiful gift of God, which outshines the fascinations of a bad world, and which no one ever sought in sincerity and was disappointed.[121]

What a glorious vision of true Christian freedom Newman presents to us! The world wants you to believe that God's commands are obstacles to happiness, that they will detract from the fullness of life that others are experiencing and that you deserve. But this is a foul lie from the pit of hell. Mary and the saints show us that true freedom can be found only in saying, "Not my will but thine be done," and that this way of living is the royal road to authentic happiness. As the poet Charles Péguy remarked, "Life holds only one tragedy, ultimately: not to have been a saint."[122] Staking our happiness on any created good will eventually lead to misery and heartache; only union with God as a saint in heaven will bring us the happiness for which we were designed.

4

SALVATION AND THE
INDWELLING OF THE
HOLY SPIRIT

The nineteenth-century philosopher Søren Kierkegaard wrote that "purity of heart is to will one thing." When you dig into Newman's writings, you find that he possessed a similar outlook. Like Kierkegaard, Newman recognized that one of the major hurdles in the journey toward God is a divided heart. This must have been an occasional struggle in Newman's own life, because he penned a prayer specifically asking for the grace to desire God alone:

> My God, how far am I from acting according to what I know so well! I confess it, my heart goes after shadows. I love anything better than com-

munion with Thee. I am ever eager to get away
from Thee. Often I find it difficult even to say
my prayers. ... Give me grace, O my Father, to
be utterly ashamed of my own reluctance! Rouse
me from sloth and coldness, and make me desire
Thee with my whole heart. ... Teach me to love
that which must engage my mind for all eternity.[123]

If a heroic saint like Newman struggled with distraction, we
should not be surprised — or driven to despair — when we do
as well. This is a common struggle in the spiritual life, and, as
Newman models for us, it demands a serious commitment to
prayer in order to be overcome.

When discussing these matters, Newman can be unsparing
in his diagnosis of our spiritual condition. After the sin of our
first parents, our default status, he says, is one of resistance toward God. "We have stony hearts," Newman observes, "hearts as
hard as the highways. ... And yet, if we would be saved, we must
have tender, sensitive, living hearts."[124] The problem, though, is
that we are also prone to self-reliance. With the first stirrings
of divine grace in our hearts, we may begin to desire God, but
so often we forge ahead on our own rather than patiently relying upon God to perform the work that needs to be done. Such
a strategy is just as foolish as trying to perform major surgery
upon oneself, when only the skilled hand of an expert surgeon
can make one whole.

Besides having a heart of stone, or perhaps closely related to
it, we tend to want the rewards of heaven without undergoing
the sacrifices that following Christ demands. This disposition
is fundamentally a sin of pride. When we go this route, we fall
into the trap of the prodigal son, who prematurely requested the
inheritance that would rightfully belong to him upon his father's
death. In effect, by demanding his inheritance, the prodigal son
was saying to his father, "I wish you would drop dead." The

prodigal son at the start of the parable is like us when we can see the goal of the beatific vision but look around for some shortcut to get there — a path to glory, in other words, that bypasses the cross.

Newman speaks to this spiritual malady as well. "We do not like to be new-made," he points out. "We are afraid of it; it is throwing us out of all our natural ways, of all that is familiar to us. We feel as if we should not *be* ourselves any longer, if we do not keep some portion of what we have been hitherto."[125] The stubbornness that Newman talks about here is a widespread mindset in our day. In a homily in 2005, Pope Benedict XVI cast a light on this problem. Pope Benedict's thoughts in that reflection have a very Newmanesque tone to them:

> Are we not perhaps all afraid in some way? If we let Christ enter fully into our lives, if we open ourselves totally to him, are we not afraid that He might take something away from us? Are we not perhaps afraid to give up something significant, something unique, something that makes life so beautiful? Do we not then risk ending up diminished and deprived of our freedom?

The questions that Pope Benedict poses in this homily nag incessantly at the human heart. Particularly if our gaze is outward, at the parties and great times that "everyone else" is enjoying, we worry that taking up our cross will mean missing out on some facet of life that is integral to happiness. But, in Benedict's view, the answer to the questions he asks is obvious. Addressing specifically the young people in the audience, he continues:

> No! If we let Christ into our lives, we lose nothing, nothing, absolutely nothing of what makes life free, beautiful and great. No! Only in this friendship are the doors of life opened wide. Only

in this friendship is the great potential of human existence truly revealed. Only in this friendship do we experience beauty and liberation. And so, today, with great strength and great conviction, on the basis of long personal experience of life, I say to you, dear young people: Do not be afraid of Christ! He takes nothing away, and he gives you everything. When we give ourselves to him, we receive a hundredfold in return. Yes, open, open wide the doors to Christ — and you will find true life. Amen.[126]

Benedict turns our anxiety about loss on its head: far from taking something away from life, Christ is, in reality, the only source of true and lasting happiness. We lose nothing in giving ourselves to him; quite the opposite: we receive far more than our hearts could ever imagine.

Being "new-made," however, is a work that only God can do, and it is not without some pain. "What ... is it that we who profess religion lack?" Newman asks. It is this: "a willingness to be changed, a willingness to suffer ... Almighty God to change us. We do not like to let go our old selves," Newman continues, so we resist the surgical hand of God.[127]

In his fantasy novel *The Voyage of the Dawn Treader*, C. S. Lewis (1898–1963) provides a memorable picture of what we must undergo in order to be transformed from our old self into a new self. Midway through the story, one of the main characters, a precocious adolescent named Eustace, discovers a cave filled with treasure that is guarded by a fierce dragon. Upon witnessing the death of the dragon, Eustace hurriedly begins stuffing his pockets full of treasure, all the while scheming about how he can keep his newfound wealth a secret. He ends up falling asleep in the cave and then wakes up several hours later, surprised to discover that he has been magically turned into a dragon himself. This turn of events, it appears, is the punishment for his greed.

Alone and depressed, Eustace doesn't know what to do with himself, until he is beckoned by a majestic lion. Readers who are familiar with Lewis's Chronicles of Narnia will immediately recognize the lion as Aslan, the Christ figure in the imaginary world of Narnia. Aslan eventually directs Eustace to a bubbling well with marble steps leading down into the water. Upon viewing the well, Eustace feels an insatiable desire to bathe in its crystal-clear water, but the lion informs him that he must undress first. Eustace realizes that Aslan is talking about his dragon scales, and the young boy proceeds to try to descale himself (with limited success). Upon realizing that his efforts will prove vain, Eustace consents to an intervention by Aslan. Later on, Eustace narrates the experience to his companions:

> The very first tear he made was so deep that I thought it had gone right into my heart. And when he began pulling the skin off, it hurt worse than anything I've ever felt. The only thing that made me able to bear it was just the pleasure of feeling the stuff peel off. You know — if you've ever picked the scab of a sore place. It hurts like billy-oh but it *is* such fun to see it coming away. ...
>
> Well, he peeled the beastly stuff right off — just as I thought I'd done it myself the other three times, only they hadn't hurt — and there it was lying on the grass: only ever so much thicker, and darker, and more knobbly-looking than the others had been. And there was I as smooth and soft as a peeled switch and smaller than I had been. Then he caught hold of me — I didn't like that much for I was very tender underneath now that I'd no skin on — and threw me into the water. It smarted like anything but only for a moment. After that it became perfectly delicious and as soon as I started swimming and splashing

> I found that all the pain had gone from my arm.
> And then I saw why. I'd turned into a boy again.
> You'd think me simply phoney if I told you how
> I felt about my own arms. I know they've no
> muscle and are pretty mouldy compared with
> Caspian's, but I was so glad to see them.[128]

Through Aslan's intervention, Eustace is transformed from a terrible dragon into a new-made person. The transformation was absolutely necessary for Eustace to experience the happiness for which he was created, but the experience involved searing pain. Such is the nature of passing from our old way of life, as persons enslaved to sin, to new life in Christ (see Rom 6:6–11). Thankfully, God does not operate in a willy-nilly fashion, but like any good physician, has a specific plan for making us whole — namely, by gifting us with the Holy Spirit, who comes to dwell in our hearts.

THE NATURE OF JUSTIFICATION ACCORDING TO NEWMAN

Let's be honest, though: For those of us who were raised going to church, the topic of salvation can sometimes feel mundane. We hear words such as "baptism," "justification," and "eternal glory" and find that the ideas have become so familiar that they no longer move us at all. Salvation, in our minds, is a rather simple equation: human beings have sinned; God sent his Son to redeem us; by trusting in Christ's sacrifice, we are guaranteed life with God in heaven. In some instances, instead of working out our salvation with fear and trembling, as Saint Paul urges us (Phil 2:12), we may even begin to take for granted that the end result — eternal life in heaven — is all but guaranteed.

In contrast, if one digs deeply into the writings of the Christian past, one will quickly find that the question of how humans are saved is a thorny one — eliciting both awe and sometimes puzzlement on the part of great theologians. How is it, for instance, that finite creatures like ourselves not only come to know but are brought into actual communion with the infinite and all-powerful Creator of the universe? How exactly does God bridge the chasm between his eternity and our time-boundedness? And what does it look like for our lives, fraught with sin and disappointments, to be taken up into God's?

These difficult questions have sometimes led to poor answers. The theologians who have advanced erroneous ideas did not necessarily possess nefarious intentions, but in their desire to safeguard some aspect of the Christian faith, they obscured or misrepresented other important truths. Take, for instance, the monk and heretic Pelagius (c. A.D. 354–418), who was a contemporary of Saint Augustine. Pelagius was concerned that if theologians and preachers overemphasized God's grace, some Christians would think that how they lived their lives was inconsequential. In his desire to combat *antinomianism* — the rejection of any moral norms — Pelagius swung too far in the other direction, forgetting that sinful human beings are utterly lost apart from God's grace (cf. Jn 15:5). In response to Pelagius, Augustine highlighted that human beings are incapable of overcoming sin by their own efforts, though he insisted that this fact does not in any way lessen the force of the moral law.

As with Pelagius, the Protestant Reformers of the sixteenth century, out of a desire to safeguard certain important truths, ended up affirming a misguided doctrine of salvation. Martin Luther, for example, in trying to uphold that salvation was a free gift from God, ultimately claimed that we are saved by faith alone (*sola fide*) and that human beings who are mired in sin have no free will. In responding to Luther, Catholic theologians were willing to concede what he got right — salvation is a free gift of God's grace (*sola gratia*) — but insisted that this essential truth should not be taught at the expense of other key biblical affirmations, such as the teaching in the Letter of James that we are "justified by works and not by faith alone" (2:24).

Today, whether we are conscious of it or not, this history

of theological disputes can come to us as baggage, causing us to have an imbalanced approach to certain doctrinal questions or leading us to assume that we have to choose between false alternatives. Consider the following question: Is salvation a matter of placing our faith in God, or are persons considered righteous by what they do? If we are grounded in Catholic tradition, we come to realize that this way of framing the matter sets up a false dichotomy. The orthodox position is a matter of both-and. In other words, we do not have to affirm that we are saved *either* by faith *or* by works. Rather, our faith and actions work together, for just "as the body apart from the spirit is dead, so faith apart from works is dead" (Jas 2:26). We need both.

Newman's writings on justification are an excellent resource for helping us think through these questions. Because Newman had immersed himself in the theology of the early Church Fathers, he was not heavily weighed down by the baggage that I mention above. In his *Lectures on Justification*, written while he was an Anglican, Newman presents us with a compelling vision of God's grace at work in our lives. According to Newman, we are made truly holy not as a result of our efforts, but through the indwelling of the Holy Spirit, by which God imparts to us his divine nature. Through Newman's theology of justification, we will see that salvation is from beginning to end a gift of God. The gratuity of salvation, however, should not be taken to mean that we play a completely passive role in the process of being made holy. In the divine design, God graciously lifts us up to the dignity of his sons and daughters, empowering us to be co-workers in reconciling all things in Christ. If we wring our hands over whether salvation is by faith or by works — a false dichotomy in the first place — we are liable to look past the great good works that God prepared in advance for us to do (see Eph 2:10). Newman, I contend, points us in the right direction.

THE INDWELLING OF THE HOLY SPIRIT

One of the difficulties in talking about the spiritual life is the tension between our responsibility to respond to God's call and the reality that we are able to bear fruit only by abiding in Christ. Sacred Scripture is replete with challenges to turn from sin and reform our lives. "Repent and believe the good news," Jesus cries out, "for the Kingdom of God is at hand!" (Mk 1:15, ESV, slightly revised). The prophets, Saint Paul, and the book of Revelation all contain similarly urgent calls to turn from sin, but the Bible also repeatedly affirms that, as sinful human beings, we are totally dependent on God's grace. In the working out of salvation, the initiative always starts from God's side. God does not love us because we first moved toward him; rather, "while were yet sinners Christ died for us" (Rom 5:8).

Mysteriously, then, God's Word upholds both of these ideas simultaneously: God's grace makes possible our repentance, while human freedom means that we must cooperate with the grace that is made available to us. As Saint Paul memorably expresses it, "For by grace you have been saved through faith; and this is not your own doing, it is the gift of God — not because of works, lest any man should boast. For we are his workmanship, created in Christ Jesus for good works, which God prepared beforehand, that we should walk in them" (Eph 2:8–10). Our salvation is a free gift of God and not something attained by our own efforts. At the same time, we have been created to do good works; these are not incidental to the plan that God has for us. Yet even these works have been "prepared [by God] beforehand" for us to do. Elsewhere, Saint Paul admonishes Christian believers, "Work out your own salvation with fear and trembling," quickly adding, though, "for God is at work in you, both to will and to work for his good pleasure" (Phil 2:12–13). Even when it comes to working out our salvation, we confess that it is God at work within us.

We need to remind ourselves of these truths periodically, because it can be easy to fall into the trap of assuming that we will make progress in the area of discipleship if we simply apply enough elbow grease. Too often we approach spiritual growth in the same way we approach dieting and exercise: I'll see change in my life if *I* try hard enough. The results, in fact, will be proportional to *my* discipline and *my* level of sacrifice.

However well-intentioned this outlook may be, it simply does not correspond to what Sacred Scripture tells us about the dynamics of spiritual renewal. This kind of transformation demands complete reliance upon God. Again, Saint Paul: "I have been crucified with Christ; it is no longer I who live, but Christ who lives in me; and the life I now live in the flesh I live by faith in the Son of God, who loved me and gave himself for me" (Gal 2:20). The life of faith is mysteriously (yet also reassuringly) Christ working through us. The charity that is made possible through entrusting our lives to God is not something we produce on our own. It is totally a gift from above.

If all that we have been discussing is true, how are we to think about our own role in this process? Do we even have a role to play? The error that is the opposite of Pelagianism — thinking that salvation is attained by our efforts — is quietism, or apathy — i.e., assuming that we are completely passive participants in the process. It's vital, of course, that we not fall into that latter trap either. As in so many other areas, Newman offers invaluable guidance on this question. Rather than trying to make things intellectually easier by relaxing the tension, Newman affirms the mystery that is involved and then goes on to show how our renewal, or sanctification, involves a real transformation of our entire being, yet one that is from beginning to end a work of God. In short, God transforms us by coming to dwell in us, through the sending of the Holy Spirit, by whose power we are conformed to the image of Christ. This inner renewal begins at baptism, but it does not end there. It is the work of a lifetime, and one in which we never move away from our dependence on God. By coming to accept these truths, we are freed from the pressure of trying to earn God's favor. Since our sanctification rests on

God's promises and not on our willpower, we can live at peace, confident that the one "who began a good work in [us] will bring it to completion at the day of Jesus Christ" (Phil 1:6).

DEIFICATION: BECOMING PARTAKERS OF THE DIVINE NATURE

Newman's approach to justification, then, closely resembles the ancient Christian idea of *theosis*, or deification. This view of salvation has retained a steady presence in the theology of the Eastern tradition, but in the Christian West — particularly since the time of the Protestant Reformation — we have tended to think of salvation in more juridical terms.[129] As sinners, we stand guilty before God, and our justification, according to this outlook, primarily involves God's pardoning our wrongdoings, as a judge might do in a court of law. The doctrine of *theosis*, in contrast, frames salvation in medicinal terms. Sin has damaged our human nature in much the same way that disease weakens the physical body. God brings us salvation by progressively healing us from this malady. Our being made righteous, in other words, entails God's making us whole, such that we can live as we were truly created to be. A god who simply declared us healthy without restoring us to health would be no God at all.

But as Scripture indicates, this is not how our heavenly Father operates. In Saint Paul's Letter to the Galatians, for instance, we read that through baptism we are made sons and daughters of God, and thus heirs with Christ (see, Gal 4:7). By virtue of this adoption, "God has sent the Spirit of his Son into our hearts" (Gal 4:6), whereby we are made "partakers of the divine nature" (2 Pt 1:4). The indwelling of the Holy Spirit, in other words, changes our status: we move from being dead in our sins to being alive in Christ. It is as if God completely rewrites our spiritual DNA. Properly speaking, then, the source of our justification is not faith, but the presence of God dwelling within us. Faith, as Newman shows, is the result of the divine indwelling, but it is the indwelling itself that is "the real token, the real state of a justified [person]."[130] As baptized children of God, we are living tabernacles. The presence of God within us makes us truly holy and sets us apart to do God's work in the world.

Just as faith is a fruit of the Holy Spirit dwelling within us, so also is renewal. This is an important point to affirm, since, as we have seen, certain Christian traditions mistakenly assume that upholding renewal or transformation of life as essential will somehow undermine the gratuity of salvation. But that would be the case only if renewal were something that we brought about ourselves, apart from the power of God at work within us. It is not. Renewal, as with faith, is a result of God's indwelling presence. Or as Newman summarizes the matter: "Justification is wrought by the power of the Spirit, or rather by His presence within us ... faith and renewal are both present also, but as fruits of it."[131] Asking whether we are justified by faith or by works, then, is to pose the wrong question. Both are integral to our salvation, but as the fruits of justification, not as the cause of it. The cause, or "real token," of our being saved is "the presence of the Holy Ghost shed abroad in our hearts," for it is the Spirit of God who is "the Author both of faith and of renewal."[132]

If ever we have doubts about the capacity of God's presence to make us holy, we need only to turn to the pages of Sacred Scripture, which provide ample testimony to the vivifying power of the Holy Spirit. At the very beginning of God's creation of the world, the Spirit hovered over the surface of the waters (Gn 1:2). For many ancient Near Easterners, the seas were a sign of chaos and disorder — something to be feared. The Spirit's presence as described in the first chapter of the Bible signals God's command over nature as well as the Spirit's involvement in the entire creative process. Later on, when God forms the first human being from the dust of the earth, God gives life to the man by breathing into his nostrils the breath of life (Gn 2:7). The Hebrew word for "breath" in this passage is *ruach* — elsewhere translated as "spirit" or "wind" — and hearkens back to the Spirit of God (*ruach elohim*) hovering over the waters in the preceding chapter. From the creation accounts in Genesis, we see that the Spirit of God is intimately involved in the creation of all things. When Christian theologians later read these textual details alongside passages such as Psalm 33:6 — "By the *word* of the LORD the heavens were made, and all their host by the *breath* of his mouth" (emphasis added) — they naturally saw a confirmation of the trinitarian idea that Father, Son (Word), and Holy Spirit (Breath) were inseparably united in creating the world.[133]

God's creative activity, as depicted in Genesis, has an important corollary in the sacraments of the New Covenant. At each celebration of the Eucharist, the priest asks God to send down his Spirit upon the gifts, so that they might become for us the Body and Blood of Christ.[134] Through this sending of the Holy Spirit, God transforms the ordinary gifts of bread and wine into the means of our salvation, for in the reception of Holy Communion we ingest the very life of God. This sacred mystery is likely what Saint Peter has in view when he remarks that we are made "partakers of the divine nature." Our Lord himself highlights the Spirit's role in the transformation of the Eucharistic elements into his Body and Blood in the famous Bread of Life discourse of John 6. When the disciples take offense at Christ's saying that his flesh is true food and his blood true drink, Jesus responds by telling them, "It is the spirit that gives life, the flesh is of no avail; the words that I have spoken to you are spirit and life" (Jn 6:63).

These biblical and theological truths shed important light on the salvific work that God accomplishes in the lives of the elect. What takes place at each Mass when the priest, standing *in persona Christi*, calls down the Spirit upon the gifts, is analogous to what God does whenever he makes a person righteous. In human terms, the transformation of the Eucharistic elements and the act of sinners' being made righteous seem impossible. But God's activity is not limited by what is humanly possible, because his word has life-giving power. "Such is the characteristic of God's doings, as manifested in Scripture," Newman writes, "that what [humans do] by working, God does by speaking."[135] Or, as Newman pithily puts it in the preceding lecture, "God's word ... effects what it announces."[136] Just as "word and deed went together in creation ... so again 'in the regeneration.' "[137] The same God who created all that is out of nothing is more than capable of making sinners righteous. We can trust God's power to save us from our sins, because we daily see before our eyes the power of God's Word, both in the majesty of creation and in the reality of God's presence upon our altars.

We misconstrue the doctrine of justification, therefore, if we reduce it solely to a matter of God's counting sinners righteous. For as Newman points out, "to 'justify' *means* in itself 'counting righteous,' but includes *under* its meaning 'making righteous.' "[138] This broader range of the term beyond what Protestant Christians sometimes give to it makes sense in light of what we have seen above about the power inherent in God's spoken word. Humans accomplish things by working; God does so by speaking. Thus, when God declares us righteous (as all Christians confess), God's word accomplishes what it declares: "If God's word and work be as closely united as action and result are in ourselves, surely as we use the word 'work' in both senses, to mean both the doing and the thing done, so we may fairly speak of justification [as referring to both] renewal, as well as mere acceptance" — to God's declaring us justified as well as our being justified.[139] In rebuttal, then, to those who would argue that God merely declares us justified while leaving us in our sinful state, Newman calmly rejoins, "Surely it is a strange paradox to say that a thing is not because [God] says it is ... that His accepting our obedience is a bar to His making it acceptable, and that the glory of His pronouncing us righteous lies in His leaving us unrighteous."[140] The theology of salvation by faith alone, in its bracketing of the renewal brought about by God's indwelling presence, does not end up safeguarding the notion of divine initiative — as it intends to do — but inadvertently obscures the power of God's Word to effect what it declares.

LIFE IN THE SPIRIT

This chapter is admittedly more speculative than what we discussed previously. And by this point, you might be asking: What does understanding the nature of justification have to do with living the Christian life? The short answer is *everything.* Once we see how God's word spoken over our lives is powerful to make us righteous, we are freed from the pressure of attaining holiness through our own efforts. While we are not passive instruments in the process, the real source of our strength is always ultimately God. Losing sight of this truth will only breed a perpetual cycle of guilt and frustration on our part. Apart from Christ we can do nothing; through his power, we can accomplish all things (see Jn 15:5 and Phil 4:13).

As intimated above, the saint is analogous to the consecrated bread and wine that have been blessed by a priest at Mass. What gives these ordinary elements the extraordinary power to save us is precisely the working of the Holy Spirit, who transforms them into instruments of God's grace. So it is with those who have been called according to God's purpose and plan. By the sending of the Holy Spirit into our hearts (Rom 5:5), God elevates our human nature to a supernatural end, such that we are made "sacraments" of his presence in the world. Corporately, the baptized faithful make up the Body of Christ, or the community of faith, which the bishops at Vatican II described as "the universal sacrament of salvation."[141] In other words, the Church is like a sacrament in that she serves as a vehicle of God's saving presence to all peoples. What a tremendous vocation: as individual persons, to be temples of the Holy Spirit and, together, operating as the Body of Christ in the world!

In line with his outlook on deification, Newman consistently supplements his ethical admonitions with reminders that we need to ask God for an increase of the Holy Spirit's influence on our lives. Again, the Christian life is not a matter of pulling ourselves up by the bootstraps but of allowing the Spirit, who is present within us, to guide every facet of our existence. True renewal begins with recognizing one's own powerlessness — "I beg Thee, O my dear Savior, to recover me!" Newman prays. "Thy grace alone can do it. I cannot save myself"[142] — and is carried out by daily submitting one's will to the leading of the Holy Spirit. As we grow in the life of the Spirit, we will find ourselves ever more ready to pray as Newman did:

> My most Holy Lord and Sanctifier, whatever there is of good in me is Thine. Without Thee, I should but get worse and worse as years went on, and should tend to be a devil. If I differ at all from the world, it is because Thou hast chosen me out of the world, and hast lit up the love of God in my heart. If I differ from Thy Saints, it is because I do not ask earnestly enough for Thy grace, and for enough of it, and because I do not diligently improve what Thou hast given me. Increase in me this grace of love, in spite of all my unworthiness. It is more precious than anything else in the world. I accept it in place of all the world can give me. O give it to me! It is my life.[143]

This is the vision of life that we must develop if we are going to cultivate an active reliance upon God. As we begin to see the grace of God's love as "more precious than anything else in the world," we will progressively develop a revulsion for anything that would kill that grace within us. The world, Newman warns, "thinks sin the same sort of imperfection as an impropriety, or want of taste or as an infirmity."[144] In contrast, those whose vision has been transformed by faith are able to see sin as God sees it. Why did the eternal Son of God deign to suffer such "unheard of and extreme torments?" Because of sin, Newman reminds us — your sin and mine. By meditating on the cross, we "learn how great an evil sin is. The death of the Infinite is its sole measure."[145] How could we go on sinning in possession of such knowledge?

Part of the "mystery of iniquity," it seems, is that so many of us do go on sinning. Even so great a figure as Saint Paul found himself mystified by the weight of concupiscence on his soul: "I do not understand my own actions. For I do not do what I want, but I do the very thing I hate" (Rom 7:15). In this passage from Romans, Paul highlights the challenge of living in a world impacted by sin. In his letter to the Galatians he recommends a way forward. Paul's word to the Galatians is not "try harder" but "walk by the Spirit, and you will not gratify the desires of the flesh" (5:16, NIV). Notice the order in which Paul places these two ideas. He does not say, "Refuse to gratify the desires of the flesh, and you will have the Holy Spirit within you." But, instead, he leads with the charge to "walk by the Spirit" and is convinced that righteous living will naturally follow. In other words, become what you already are, that is, a temple of the Holy Spirit. It's not surprising, then, that Paul refers to the moral dispositions of love, joy, peace, patience, and so forth as "fruit of the Spirit," because these characteristics are not naturally produced by sinful human beings. Rather, they are the supernatural effects of God's Spirit dwelling within us.

In this area, then, Newman's theology is robustly Pauline. For Newman, sin represents not an inferior choice, or a matter of taste, but something wholly irrational, because it strikes against the very notion of who God created us to be. As the first chapters of Genesis indicate, we are God's image bearers, designed to live in intimate communion with our Creator. Though sin ruptured this communion, God has not left us to our own devices but has sent his Son, Our Lord Jesus Christ, through whom we have now received reconciliation (Rom 5:11). The reconciliation that we presently experience, as members of Christ's Body, is a foretaste of eternal beatitude. The Holy Spirit's indwelling, in this sense, is a "down payment" of the full communion that awaits us when God restores all things in Christ. As Saint Paul says, God has "put his seal upon us and given us his Spirit in our hearts as a guarantee" (2 Cor 1:22). In light of the Spirit's presence within us, sin cannot but appear incomprehensible. Newman prays:

> O my God, can I sin when Thou art within me
> so intimately? Can I forget who is with me, who
> is in me? Can I expel a Divine Inhabitant by that
> which He abhors more than anything else, which
> is the one thing in the whole world which is of-
> fensive to Him, the only thing which is not His?
> ... My God, I have a double security against sin-
> ning; first the dread of such a profanation of all
> Thou art to me in Thy very Presence; and next
> because I do trust that that Presence will preserve
> me from sin. My God, Thou wilt go from me, if
> I sin; and I shall be left to my own miserable self.
> God forbid! I will use what Thou hast given me;
> I will call on Thee when tried and tempted. ...
> Through Thee I will never forsake Thee.[146]

Let us ask God, then, for the full measure of the "double security" to which Newman refers, that we might come to abhor sin as much as the body rejects poison. In developing this abhorrence for sin, may we not trust in our own strength but rely solely on the Paraclete whom God has sent as an Advocate on our behalf (see Jn 14:15–18):

> My God, the Paraclete, I acknowledge Thee as
> the Giver of that great gift, by which alone we are
> saved, supernatural love. Man is by nature blind
> and hardhearted in all spiritual matters; how is
> he to reach heaven? It is by the flame of Thy grace,
> which consumes him in order to new-make him,
> and so to fit him to enjoy what without Thee he
> would have no taste for. ... By Thee we wake up
> from the death of sin, to exchange the idolatry of
> the creature for the pure love of the Creator. ...

> By the fire which Thou didst kindle within us, we
> pray, and meditate, and do penance. As well could
> our bodies live, if the sun were extinguished, as
> our souls, if Thou art away.[147]

CONCLUSION: FROM FIRST TO LAST, THE GIFT OF GOD

Newman's theology of the Holy Spirit, outlined above, provides us with a richer understanding of how salvation truly is a gift from God. In the wake of the Protestant Reformation, theologians of all stripes have arguably focused too much on the question of faith versus works viewed as actions that human beings perform. In contrast, Newman repeatedly brings the conversation back to the primacy of God's action. Stated succinctly, our understanding of salvation is likely to be off if we begin with the role that human beings play rather than with the divine initiative. Furthermore, we can properly understand our involvement only if we view it against the backdrop of God's initiative. As Newman emphasizes, both our faith and our works are the fruit of the Holy Spirit dwelling within us, not realities that we are able to produce by our own effort. In scriptural language, "We love, because [God] first loved us" (1 Jn 4:19).

This theme is a consistent thread running throughout Newman's preaching. In a later Catholic sermon, for instance, he notes that, "There is no truth ... which Holy Church is more earnest in impressing upon us than that our salvation from first to last is the gift of God. It is true indeed that we merit eternal life by our works of obedience; but that those works are meritorious of such a reward, this takes place, not from their intrinsic worth, but from the free appointment and bountiful promise of God; and that we are able to do them at all, is the simple result of His grace."[148] Of course, in emphasizing that salvation is a gift, we should be careful not to understand this idea in such a way that we deny the reality of human free will. As Newman reminds us, "Precise and absolute as is the teaching of Holy Church concerning the sovereign grace of God, she is as clear and as earnest in teaching also that we are really free and responsible."[149] Undoubtedly, there will always remain a degree of mystery here, but Newman thinks it important that we not collapse the tension in order to provide an answer suitable to human understanding.

Without in any way denying human freedom, then, Newman goes on to say that our hope ultimately rests on who God is and what he has promised us. As to the former, we confess that God "is the Alpha and Omega, the beginning and the ending, as of all things, so of our salvation."[150] Apart from a "gift which we could not do anything ourselves to secure," every one of us would die "destitute of all saving knowledge and love of Him."[151] This truth applies not only to our initiation into the life of grace but, in fact, to the entire order of salvation. Our knowledge of God is a result of God's self-revelation; we are cleansed from our sins by the operation of sacramental grace; and our perseverance in holiness is through the help of the Holy Spirit. As Newman summarizes the matter, "[God's] grace begins the work, His grace also finishes it."[152]

Besides being a source of consolation to us, this truth should also inform how we go about praying and practicing works of mercy. There is an old saying, sometimes attributed to Saint Ignatius of Loyola, that recommends: "Pray as though everything depended on God; act as though everything depended on you." Taking seriously the second half of this quote, we ought to be intentional about setting goals, practicing self-denial, and sharing God's love with others. Nevertheless, we demonstrate our trust in God by regularly turning to God in prayer to ask for the grace of perseverance. No matter how far we progress in the spiritual life, we never move beyond our need for this grace. As Newman says, "In spite of the presence of grace in our souls … we owe any hope we have of heaven, not to that inward grace simply" but "to a supplementary mercy which protects us against ourselves, rescues us from occasions of sin, [and] strengthens us in our hour of danger."[153] To state the matter somewhat paradoxically, we use our freedom best when we use it to plead with God for the grace of final perseverance, knowing full well that apart from this "supplementary mercy" we would be ruined.

Newman ends this sermon with a beautiful meditation on the communion of saints. As with so many of his sermons, Newman here skillfully weaves together the radical challenge of the Gospel call with the consolation that comes with knowing the full measure of God's grace. The intercession of the saints is one of the most palpable manifestations of God's concern for us. Since God has given us Mary as our mother and the saints as our brothers and sisters, we ought to be diligent in asking for their prayers. Or as Newman counsels: "Interest your dear Mother, the Mother of God, in your success; pray to her earnestly for it; she can do more for you than any one else."[154] A strong relationship with Mary and the saints will be a source of great comfort to us when we come to face our final trial, at the hour of death:

> It will be most blessed, when the evil one is making his last effort, when he is coming on you in his might to pluck you away from your Father's hand, if he can — it will be blessed indeed if Jesus, if Mary and Joseph are then with you, waiting to shield you from his assaults and to receive your soul. If they are there, all are there; Angels are there, Saints are there, heaven is there, heaven is begun in you, and the devil has no part in you.[155]

If you are unsure about where to begin in terms of asking for the grace of final perseverance, may I suggest making the Rosary a part of your daily prayer life? According to Newman, "The great power of the Rosary lies in this, that it makes the Creed into a prayer; of course, the Creed is in some sense a prayer and a great act of homage to God; but the Rosary gives us the great truths of [Christ's] life and death to meditate upon, and brings them nearer to our hearts."[156] Furthermore, as Saint Alphonsus

Liguori reminds us, "the Lord has ordained that all graces shall pass through Mary, as a channel of mercy."[157] It should not surprise us, then, that (as a priest once told me) "all the Saints have a Marian modality." We need to have one as well.

5
FIXING OUR EYES ON JESUS

There is a certain tension at the heart of Christian discipleship. On the one hand, Jesus sets extraordinarily high ethical demands for his followers: turn the other cheek, lend without expecting anything in return, be perfect as your Heavenly Father is perfect, and so on. On the other hand, the overall New Testament vision for sanctification is not focused on human effort. The goal, rather, is to have one's life subsumed into the person of Jesus, such that one is able to say (as Saint Paul did), "I have been crucified with Christ; it is no longer I who live, but Christ who lives in me; and the life I now live in the flesh I live by faith in the Son of God, who loved me and gave himself for me" (Gal 2:20). In persons who consistently cooperate with God's grace, it is as if Christ is operating directly through their activity in the world.

The twelfth chapter of Hebrews succinctly expresses this tension between our free response to God's call and the reality that we are dependent on divine empowerment. The author instructs the recipients of the letter to "run with perseverance the race that is set before us" — so the impetus to endure appears to fall on us — but then he quickly adds, "looking to Jesus the pioneer and perfecter of our faith" (vv. 1–2). In other words, the secret to persevering is not to focus inward, on the self, but to keep our vision fixed upon Jesus. As Newman pithily summarizes the matter, "Surely it is our duty ever to look off ourselves, and to look unto Jesus."[158]

A friend recently told me that whenever he reads an article in a Catholic magazine, he counts how many times the piece mentions Jesus. This friend has a sneaking suspicion that too many Catholics, even those who write regularly about faith, are drifting away from a sense of how central Christ is to our faith. We sometimes write about environmentalism, sexual morality, the economy, and a host of other topics, but without connecting the conversation in some way to our most fundamental commitment of following Jesus. Now, one could certainly go overboard with insisting too strongly on this point: There are no doubt occasions when it's appropriate to discuss a certain issue within the framework of a field other than theology. Nevertheless, I think my friend is onto something in pressing that Catholics need to be more intentional about keeping Jesus at the center of our conversations about the most important matters in life.

Saint John Henry could never be accused of speaking too little about Jesus. In his various writings, he developed a profound Christology, and a significant number of his sermons take as their starting point the commands and example of Christ. For Newman, as with the authors of the New Testament, one way of describing holiness is quite simply as total conformity to Christ. The Incarnate Word of God, in his earthly life, showed us definitively what it means to be human, and if we are to reach the destiny that God has prepared for us, our focus must always remain on the way of life that Jesus modeled for us. In this respect, Newman's outlook closely tracks with that of Saint Irenaeus, who remarked that "the glory of God is a human being fully alive!" In other words, we exhibit God's glory most brilliantly when our life resembles as closely as possible the life of Jesus, because the Son of God's embodied existence *is* what it looks like to be fully alive. Newman recognized this truth and, through his preaching, left behind a treasure trove of insights about imitating Christ.

CONTEMPLATING THE PERSON OF CHRIST

The foundation of Newman's Christ-centered spirituality was his contention that the doctrines concerning Jesus matter not simply for our understanding of how God saves us but also for how we live our daily existence. During his Anglican days, Newman was particularly concerned that Evangelicals in England were emphasizing the doctrine of the atonement to the detriment of other important truths. In his view, the popular religion of the day gave "disproportionate attention to the doctrines connected with the work of Christ, in comparison of those which relate to His Person."[159] As a consequence, "the rich and varied Revelation of our merciful Lord" — including all that we learn about Jesus in the Gospels — was "practically reduced [by Evangelicals] to a few chapters of St Paul's Epistles."[160] In their haste to defend the theory of justification by faith alone, Evangelicals arguably paid more attention to the content of Paul's letters than to the Gospels themselves.[161]

Newman, of course, had no intention of denigrating the doctrine of the atonement. He insisted, though, that this truth of the Faith must always be viewed in its relation to other key teachings concerning Jesus. We must, therefore, keep before our eyes both Jesus' work *and* his person. What concerns us as Christians is not simply Our Lord's death on the cross, but also what "Scripture has set ... before us [as to] His actual sojourn on earth ... His gestures, words, and deeds."[162] Newman urges us, then, to move beyond "a mere idea" of our Savior so as to "contemplate Christ as manifested in the Gospels, the Christ who exists therein, external to our own imaginings" — i.e., the living, flesh-and-blood person who healed the sick, proclaimed freedom for captives, and preached good news to the poor (see Lk 4:16–21).[163]

Ultimately, for Newman, the Incarnation — the mystery of the Divine Word made flesh — represents "the central truth of the gospel."[164] And the Incarnation encompasses more than simply Christ's death on Calvary. It also encompasses his birth in Bethlehem, the totality of his teaching ministry, and his glorious resurrection and ascension into heaven. Each of these facets of the Incarnation contains vital insights regarding the shape of our life in Christ. As Newman comments, "Every passage in the history of our Lord and Savior is of unfathomable depth, and affords inexhaustible matter of contemplation."[165] By unfolding the significance of these mysteries, Newman seeks to set forth Christ, first and foremost, "as the object of our worship," but also as the exemplar whom we are called to imitate.[166]

OMNIPOTENCE IN BONDS

One of the ways that Newman unfolds the mystery of the Incarnation is by bringing to the fore Christ's divine nature. In Newman's view, reminding ourselves of Jesus' full divinity provides a different perspective on the events that occurred in his life. Consider, for instance, the Passion of Our Lord, which Newman reflects on at length in a sermon titled "The Incarnate Son, a Sufferer and Sacrifice." On a merely human level, we might be moved by hearing of an innocent man wrongly arrested, tortured, and condemned to die. But these events take on a whole new light when we reflect on the fact that it was God the Son whom Roman authorities executed at Calvary: "That Face, so ruthlessly smitten, was the Face of God Himself; the Brows bloody with the thorns, the sacred Body exposed to view and lacerated with the scourge, the Hands nailed to the Cross, and, afterwards, the Side pierced with the spear; it was the Blood, and the sacred Flesh, and the Hands, and the Temples, and the Side, and the Feet of God Himself, which the frenzied multitude then gazed upon."[167] It is a fearful thought, Newman says, to recognize what really took place at Christ's crucifixion. This was no mere mortal who died; it was "Almighty God Himself, God the Son, [who] was the Sufferer" and the sacrifice.[168]

This "mystery of divine condescension," though it shines forth preeminently in Jesus' death on the cross, was characteristic of Our Lord's entire earthly existence, beginning with the very moment of his conception.[169] "When the Eternal son of God came among us," Newman observes, "He might have taken our nature, as Adam received it, from the earth, and have begun His human life at [a] mature age; He might have been molded under the immediate hand of the Creator; He need have known nothing of the feebleness of infancy or the slow growth of manhood."[170] But that was not the path Christ chose. Instead, "infinity was dwindled to infancy."[171] The Eternal Word of God — all-powerful and in need of nothing — became flesh and was contained within the womb of a woman. As a shorthand reference for this mystery, Newman speaks of "Omnipotence in bonds": "the All-powerful, the All-free, the Infinite, became and becomes, as the text says, 'subject' to the creature; nay, not only a subject, but literally a captive, a prisoner, and that not once, but on many different occasions and in many different ways."[172]

Newman proceeds to elaborate on several of these ways. "The standing mystery of Omnipotence in bonds" that began with Christ's conception was carried forward in his submission to the customs and the rituals of his people, most notably in his undergoing the rite of circumcision.[173] It was evident as well in the obedience and respect that he gave to his parents. Until the age of thirty, for instance, Christ confined himself to the limits of one city, humbly working at his father's trade. The most arresting display of Omnipotence in bonds was Christ's willingly suffering a painful, humiliating death. In Newman's interpretation, "that sacrifice of Himself" would not have been pleasing to Christ unless it involved "imprisonment." Therefore,

Our Lord "allowed Himself in the Church's words, '*manibus tradi nocentium*,' to be given into the hands of the violent."[174] What a profound mystery, that the Second Person of the Trinity, the one through whom all things were made (see Jn 1:3), would turn himself over to unjust men in order to be tortured and put to death.

Amazingly, the Son of God's subjection to creatures did not cease even after his resurrection — as we might expect it to. For the Holy Eucharist, Newman points out, extends this mystery into the age of the Church. As Newman puts it, Christ sets "such a value on subjection to His creatures, that, before He goes away, on the very eve of His betrayal, He ... actually make[s] provision, after death, for perpetuating His captivity to the end of the world."[175] Newman's commentary on this point powerfully illumines what takes place at each Mass:

> My Brethren, the great truth is daily before our eyes: He has ordained the standing miracle of His Body and Blood under visible symbols, that He may secure thereby the standing mystery of Omnipotence in bonds. He took bread, and blessed, and made it His Body; He took wine, and gave thanks, and made it His Blood; and He gave His priests the power to do what He had done. Henceforth, He is in the hands of sinners once more. Frail, ignorant, sinful man, by the sacerdotal power given to him, compels the presence of the Highest; he lays Him up in a small tabernacle; he dispenses Him to a sinful people. Those who are only just now cleansed from mortal sin, open their lips for Him; those who are soon to return to mortal sin, receive Him into their breasts; those who are polluted with vanity and selfishness and ambition and pride, presume to make Him their guest; the frivolous, the tepid, the world-

ly-minded, fear not to welcome Him. Alas! alas!
even those who wish to be more in earnest, en-
tertain Him with cold and wandering thoughts,
and quench that Love which would inflame them
with Its own fire, did they but open to It.[176]

Clearly, we serve a God who does not remain distant from
his creatures but draws near to them — draws near to *us* —
through acts of condescension that are difficult for us even to
comprehend. As human beings, when we think about omnipotence, our minds naturally go to the idea of limitless strength.
But, as Newman reminds us, to think about omnipotence in
those terms is to gain only "a half-knowledge" of God. The other
side of God's omnipotence is that it can "swathe Itself in infirmity and can become the captive of Its own creatures."[177] In a wonderful turn of phrase, Newman remarks that God possesses "the
incomprehensible power of even making Himself weak," such
that to know God perfectly, we must know him as Immanuel, or
"God with us."[178]

THE IMITATION OF CHRIST

For Newman, meditation on the person and work of Christ is
never simply a matter of abstract theological speculation. To
the contrary, we as Christians are called to mold our lives after
the concrete shape of Jesus' example of humility and self-sacrifice. To be precise, we must admit, as Newman does, that there
was something unique about the Passion and death of Christ.
As Newman puts it, "Christ's death was not a mere martyr-
dom. A martyr is one who dies for the Church ... but [Jesus]
was much more than a Martyr."[179] Human beings die as martyrs, but Christ, being fully divine, died as an atoning sacrifice.
Thus, "there was a virtue in His death, which there could be in
no other, for He was God."[180] Nevertheless, as followers of Jesus, we have been called to take up our crosses, in our own way,
and thereby to give witness to the world about the love that has

transformed our lives. For this reason, the martyrs are given special honor in the Christian faith, for in their fidelity to the Gospel, they conformed as closely as was humanly possible to the self-sacrificial love that was embodied perfectly in Jesus.

Newman's vision of the imitation of Christ closely resembles the theological outlook of Saint Paul. In his letter to the church at Philippi, Paul provides a stirring account of how our lives are meant to conform to Christ's:

> Do nothing from selfishness or conceit, but in humility count others better than yourselves. Let each of you look not only to his own interests, but also to the interests of others. Have this mind among yourselves, which was in Christ Jesus, who, though he was in the form of God, did not count equality with God a thing to be grasped, but emptied himself, taking the form of a servant, being born in the likeness of men. And being found in human form he humbled himself and became obedient unto death, even death on a cross. (Phil 2:3–8)

Newman memorably captures this same constellation of ideas by describing the cross of Christ as "the measure of the world," "the *heart* of religion."[181] Regarding this second phrase, Newman notes that, "The heart may be considered as the seat of life; it is the principle of motion, heat, and activity. ... It sustains the [person] in his powers and faculties; it enables the brain to think; and when it is touched, man dies."[182] Analogously, "the sacred doctrine of Christ's Atoning Sacrifice is the vital principle on which the Christian lives, and without which Christianity is not."[183] Christ's death on the cross is not only the fulcrum upon which all of human history turns; it is the very heart of our existence as baptized members of his body.

What does the above mean in practical terms for our daily walk as Christians? As a starting point, Newman observes that "the heart is hidden from view; it is carefully and securely guarded; it is not like the eye set in the forehead, commanding all, and seen of all; and so in like manner the sacred doctrine of the Atoning Sacrifice is not one to be talked of, but to be lived upon."[184] He then warns that if we live our lives carelessly while paying lip service to the cross, we actually cast aspersion on the work that Christ has accomplished. There will undoubtedly be times when we are called upon to communicate verbally the significance of Christ's death, but preeminently Our Lord's Passion is meant to serve as the heart of our lived practice, pumping life into every facet of our daily existence. As examples of when it is prudent to speak of Christ's atoning sacrifice, Newman points to the ministries of catechesis, educating young children, comforting the sorrowful, and guiding sinners who are earnestly seeking a rule of life.[185] These are all persons who can benefit from looking to the cross as a means of cultivating faith, hope, and charity. In other contexts, we should practice a level of reserve without, of course, assuming that we must always remain silent.

From all that has been said above, we see that the doctrines of the Incarnation and the humiliation of the Eternal Son are not "abstract, speculative, and unprofitable," but are "especially practical."[186] When the truths about Christ appear disconnected from the rest of life, the problem is not with the content of the teachings but with how we have received — or failed to receive — that content. "In what true sense do we 'know' [Jesus]," Newman asks, "if our idea of Him be not such as to take up and incorporate into itself the manifold attributes and offices which we ascribe to Him? What do we gain from words, however correct and abundant, if they end with themselves instead of lighting up the image of the Incarnate Son in our hearts?"[187] As Newman emphasizes here, Christological doctrines are not meant primarily to serve as head knowledge. This knowledge, in fact, is all but useless if it does not penetrate our hearts. As the Letter of James reminds us: "Even the demons believe [that

God is one] — and shudder" (2:19). Our belief, to be saving, must issue forth into a life of charity.

Throughout his sermons, then, Newman consistently presses his fellow believers to make real their convictions about Christ by imitating his example in their daily lived existence. As a barometer for discipleship, Newman suggests that we weigh our actions against the servanthood that Christ modeled, as, for instance, when he washed his disciples' feet. That kind of servanthood is the measure of true faith, as opposed to "book knowledge," which remains in the head only. As Newman summarizes:

> True faith teaches us to do numberless disagreeable things for Christ's sake, to bear petty annoyances, which we find written down in no book. In most books Christian conduct is made grand, elevated, and splendid; so that any one, who only knows of true religion from books, and not from actual endeavors to be religious, is sure to be offended at religion when he actually comes upon it, from the roughness and humbleness of his duties, and his necessary deficiencies in doing them. It is beautiful in a picture to wash the disciples' feet; but the sands of the real desert have no lustre in them to compensate for the servile nature of the occupation.[188]

When our hearts become inflamed with the image of the Incarnate Son, we are willing to accept the most menial of tasks in imitation of the humility and servant example of Our Lord. In contrast, if our faith stays at the level of head knowledge, we are likely to conclude (mistakenly!) that the life of discipleship involves only what is "grand" and "elevated." As Newman points out, though, there is nothing particularly elevated about stooping to wash the feet of sinners or with patiently bearing wrongs. We embrace such servile actions not because they are grand but because only in these ways can we truly come to know and participate in the saving Passion of Our Lord.

Examples from Newman's writings could be multiplied many times over. Again and again, he circles back to the idea of Christ's self-emptying love, because he is convinced that Jesus' exemplification of divine charity reveals the true nature of authentic human existence. The world does not know this love and even openly mocks it. In Newman's words, "What a very different view of life do these doctrines present to us from that which the world takes."[189] Whereas Jesus, though Lord of all, made himself subject to human authorities — even turning himself over as a prisoner to unjust men — "the spirit of the world" prizes autonomy, self-assertion, and pride (see 1 Cor 2). As children of God, however, we have been called to a different way of life. We have been called to imitate the Son of God's meekness and subjection to others — all of those humiliations that Newman places under the heading of "Omnipotence in bonds."

In light of Jesus' resignation to the will of the Father ("not my will but thine be done"), we ought to be ashamed of our stubborn resistance to the difficulties that providence permits us to experience. The end goal, of course, is not to wallow in shame. Ultimately, Newman sets before us the teachings and example of Christ for the sake of spurring us to repentance, so that we might set out on a different way of life:

> O my Brethren, let us blush at our own pride and self-will. Let us call to mind our impatience at God's providences towards us, our wayward longings after what cannot be, our headstrong efforts to reverse His just decrees, our bootless conflicts with the stern necessities which hem us in, our irritation at ignorance or suspense about His will, our fierce, passionate willfulness when we see that will too clearly, our haughty contempt of His ordinances, our determination to do

things for ourselves without Him, our preference
of our own reason to His word — the many, many
shapes in which the Old Adam shows itself, and
one or other of which our conscience tells us is
our own; and let us pray Him who is independent
of us all, yet who at this season [of Ephiphany-
tide] became as though our fellow and our servant, to teach us our place in His wide universe,
and to make us ambitious only of that grace here
and glory hereafter, which He has purchased for
us by His own humiliation.[190]

Setting aside all pride and self-will, let us — as Newman
prays — be ambitious in one way only: to cooperate fully with
God's grace now, so that we might have some share in God's
glory in the age to come.

6

NEWMAN ON PRAYER

Abandonment to divine providence is one of the central themes in Newman's spirituality. Our lives are not our own; they belong to God, the all-knowing Creator. Our heavenly Father knows what is best for us and, in his infinite mercy, has prepared the graces necessary for us to be made holy and reach heaven. True happiness and true peace, then, can be found only by humbly submitting our wills to God's plan. Insofar as we resist this plan, we will find ourselves more deeply mired in dissatisfaction and resentment.

The notion of abandoning oneself to divine providence can be a topic that is easy to write about but exceedingly difficult to practice in real life. When life is proceeding smoothly, with fulfilling relationships and our material needs provided for, it can seem simple enough to submit to God's will. But inevitably the storms of life arise, and then our faith is tested. When our bank account dries up, when a loved one is diagnosed with cancer, when our own health begins to fail: In these and similar situations saying, "Not my will but thine be done," can feel difficult if not impossible to do.

From Newman's vantage point, this is one of the reasons why prayer is so vital to growth in the spiritual life. We cannot abandon ourselves to divine providence, he observes, simply by wishing for the desire to do so. Submitting oneself entirely to God's will is a habit that is acquired over time, through many small self-denials, but this asceticism also has to be grounded in a consistent prayer life. Only through the discipline of regular prayer can we learn to hear the Shepherd's voice and, in turn, to recognize that God is the One who is ultimately in charge of our lives. "Many are the plans in the mind of a person, but it is the purpose of the LORD that will be established" (Prv 19:21, slightly altered).

It's completely foolhardy, then, to imagine ourselves growing in faith, hope, and love apart from daily conversation with God. On this topic, Newman is as forthright as possible, so that his readers will have no chance of overlooking what is at stake in turning to prayer. "Prayer and fasting," he writes, "have been called the wings of the soul, and they who neither fast nor pray, cannot follow Christ. They cannot lift up their hearts to Him."[191] In this evocative image, our souls without prayer are like birds with clipped wings. We may long to soar above the clouds — to know experientially the riches of God's glory — but we will remain grounded for as long as we close ourselves off to "divine converse."[192]

To add another layer to this conversation, can you imagine someone who is horribly out of shape planning to run a marathon without altering his unhealthful eating habits or sedentary lifestyle? If you met such a person, you would likely think he was insane. Deep down — notwithstanding the promises of wonder-working diet pills — we all know that when it comes to physical fitness, there are no easy shortcuts or quick fixes. Losing weight and becoming faster and stronger require serious discipline and concrete sacrifices. That being the case, why do we so often assume that things will somehow be different in the spiritual life? Saint Paul informs us that, "while bodily training is of some value, godliness is of value in every way, as it holds promise for the present life and also for the life to come" (1 Tm 4:8). In other words, our spiritual well-being is of far greater value than our physical fitness. Indeed, it is of inestimable value. With that in view, we should expect that the training required for godliness will require a greater level of sacrifice than what it takes to get in shape physically.

In fact, Newman takes this entire conversation one step further. For him, the best analogy for the importance of prayer may be not physical exercise but the basic cardiovascular processes that sustain bodily life. As he puts it, "Prayer is to spiritual life what the beating of the pulse and the drawing of the breath are to the life of the body. It would be as absurd to suppose that life could last when the body was cold and motionless and senseless, as to call a soul alive which does not pray."[193] How many of us can honestly say that we approach prayer with the urgency that Newman ascribes to it? When we neglect the spiritual discipline of prayer, we are not proving our self-sufficiency; we are demonstrating our pride. We are like walking corpses, feigning the appearance of life, when in reality there is no life within us.

DEVELOPING THE HABIT OF PRAYER

In his first letter to the church in Thessalonica, Saint Paul exhorts the Christians there to "pray without ceasing" (1 Thes 5:17, ESV). Admittedly, what Paul instructs here is a challenging command — so much so that some Christian interpreters have attempted to explain away its force, suggesting that perhaps he simply meant "pray frequently" or "pray as often as one's responsibilities permit." Newman, unsurprisingly, does not go this route. For him, "to pray always" means to have "the habit of prayer."[194] He wants to test what it would look like to fulfill this command, and the first piece of advice he gives toward this end is that we should avoid applying the text in a vague manner. From Newman's vantage point, some Christians seek to fulfill the command by bathing their daily activities with the thought of God — a worthy goal, of course — but, in the process, they neglect to set aside specific "times of private prayer."[195] In such cases, seeking to turn one's thoughts regularly to God becomes a substitute for stopping all of one's activities to focus entirely on prayer. This is a dangerous practice to fall back on, not only because it's easy for anxieties and mundane matters to crowd out the thought of God but also because human beings are notoriously prone to self-deception, and we can easily convince ourselves that we are praying more often or in a more focused manner than we actually are.

As with so many other areas of the Christian life, when it comes to prayer, Newman is refreshingly practical. The most effective foundation for a fruitful prayer life, he says, is to schedule specific times of private prayer as part of one's daily routine. Furthermore, we ought to make these times a priority rather than an afterthought. Newman specifically presses these points in the following terms:

> Give freely of your time to your Lord and Savior,
> if you have it. If you have little, show your sense
> of the privilege by giving that little. But any how,
> show that your heart and your desires, show that
> your life is with your God. Set aside every day
> times for seeking Him. ... Live by [a] rule. I am
> not calling on you to go out of the world, or to
> abandon your duties in the world, but to redeem
> the time; not to give hours to mere amusement
> or society, while you give minutes to Christ; not
> to pray to Him only when you are tired, and fit
> for nothing but sleep; not altogether to omit to
> praise Him, or to intercede for the world and the
> Church; but in good measure to realize honest-

ly the words of the text, to "set your affection on
things above;" and to prove that you are His, in
that your heart is risen with Him, and your life
hid in Him.[196]

Two things stand out in this excerpt. The first is Newman's
counsel to live by a rule. Human beings are creatures of habit,
and if we fail to set aside specific times to pray, we are unlikely
to develop the habit of praying always. Second, when it comes to
establishing set times for prayer, we should give the best of our
time to God, not the "leftovers." In my own life, I have a tendency to try to rush prayers at the end of the day and end up falling
asleep while conversing with God. Hearkening to Christ's example in the Gospels (Mk 1:35), Newman counsels, "Be up at
prayer 'a great while before the day.' "[197] This practice is akin to
giving God the "first fruits" in tithing and is the best antidote to
treating prayer as an afterthought.

Alongside establishing set times for prayer, it is also imperative, according to Newman, that we draw upon traditional devotions and "forms of prayer," by which he means prayers that
have been written for us.[198] Newman feels compelled to reinforce
this point, because he knows that there are some "self-wise rea-
soners" who think "it better to pray out of their own thoughts at
random, using words which come into their minds at the time
they pray."[199] It's easy to be swayed by such reasoning, because
many of us instinctively feel that to offer a memorized prayer
or to read a prayer out of a book is somehow less authentic in
our devotion to God. Especially in our day and age, we tend to
connect love with spontaneity, so we assume that our prayers
should naturally flow from our heart to our lips without the aid
of set words.

This assumption is a mistake, Newman asserts. We need
specific forms of prayer, and this for a few reasons. First, "forms
of prayer are necessary to guard us against the irreverence of
wandering thoughts."[200] Truth be told, wandering thoughts are

quite likely the greatest factor in derailing Christians from meaningful occasions of prayer. We are sensory creatures, and the things of this world have an immediacy that grabs our attention in a way that spiritual realities do not. Furthermore, the vast majority of us are burdened with concerns far too many to number — whether those be related to finances, health, or relationships. It's tough to focus while praying, and if we rely on extemporaneous modes of prayer alone, we make the task even more difficult. In Newman's estimation, "If we pray without set words ... our minds will stray from the subject; other thoughts will cross us, and we shall pursue them. ... This wandering of mind is in good measure prevented, under God's blessing, by forms of prayer. Thus a chief use of them is that of *fixing the attention*."[201] Rather than feeling guilty about relying on set forms of prayer, we ought to rejoice in the fact that God in his good providence has provided us with these means precisely to aid us in our weakness.

Second, these forms "are useful in securing us from the irreverence of excited thoughts."[202] With this reason, Newman turns the tables on the standard argument against such forms of prayer. As noted above, some Christian figures accuse set forms of prayer "of impeding the current of devotion," which is assumed to be of highest quality when characterized by spontaneity and unencumbered by patterns of ritual. As Newman sees the matter, though, while "there are times when a thankful or a wounded heart bursts through all forms of prayer ... these are not frequent."[203] Nor should we expect them to be, for as Newman points out, "to be excited is not the ordinary state of the mind, but the extraordinary, the now and then state."[204] Obviously, the balance between emotively expressing our desire for God and having recourse to more sober forms of prayer will be a matter of discernment in each Christian life. What Newman recognizes is that our emotions are more turbulent and, therefore, more likely to be shaped by our circumstances and present state of mind. In his view, a strong emotional response "ought not to be the common state of the mind; and if we are encouraging within us this excitement, this unceasing rush and alternation of feelings, and think that this, and this only, is being in earnest in religion, we are harming our minds, and (in one sense) I may even say grieving the peaceful Spirit of God, who would silently and tranquilly work His Divine work in our hearts."[205] The danger, then, is not in emotions per se, but in assuming that these are the only or sure sign of earnestness in religion, and thereby giving the impression that a strong emotional response is a necessary part of every prayerful experience. To prove that this is not the case, one need only point to the example of Mother Teresa, who labored for decades among the poorest of the poor, all the while struggling with a dryness of soul that looked very much like depression. If Mother Teresa had made her commitment to God dependent on emotions, she would have never accomplished the amazing work that she did on behalf of the kingdom.

Third, "forms [of prayer] are useful to help our memory, and to set before us at once, completely, and in order, what we have to pray for."[206] As Saint Paul observes, "We do not know how to pray as we ought" (Rom 8:26). As with little children, our desires get mixed up, and what we assume will make us happy may be far removed from what our heavenly Father *knows* will make us happy. By utilizing prayers that have stood the test of time, we basically set aside our own fickle desires and rely on the trustworthy wisdom that has been passed down from generation to generation. The most well-known prayers in the Catholic Tradition gained their currency precisely because the faithful came to recognize them as sure guides of God's will for our lives. The Our Father, given to us directly by Our Lord, is the preeminent example of this sort of prayer, and all other trustworthy devotions are imbued with its animating principle, expressed in the simple phrase "thy will be done."

Certainly, there are different kinds of prayer that have been utilized fruitfully by saints throughout the ages. Moreover, as one advances in the spiritual life, one is likely to become more adept at mental prayer, in which the mind ascends directly to God without slavish reliance on set forms. Nevertheless, Newman's caution is an important one. We all begin as infants in the family of God, and reaching full maturity in the life of faith requires spiritual nourishment that is suited to our capacities. As Newman reminds us, "The power of praying, being a habit, must be acquired, like all other habits, by practice."[207] This being the case, "shall we trust the matters of the next world to the chance thoughts of our own minds, which come this moment, and go the next, and may not be at hand when the time of employing them arrives, like unreal visions, having no substance and no permanence?"[208]

And here, ultimately, is the crux of the matter: "Beware lest your religion be one of sentiment merely, not of practice."[209] When we fail to schedule times of prayer and refuse to avail ourselves of the rich treasury of devotions passed down through Tradition, we risk turning our faith into a matter of sentiment and not practice. But faith, like love, is proved in deeds (not in words), and one "who does one deed of obedience for Christ's sake" — no matter how devoid of emotions — "is a better [person], and returns to his home justified rather than the most eloquent speaker, and the most sensitive hearer, of the glory of the Gospel, if such men do not practice up to their knowledge."[210] In light of what Newman says here about prayer, let us commit to being doers of the word, and not hearers only (see Jas 1:22–25) — lest we deceive ourselves and end up hardly praying at all.

Piercing through the Veil of this World
Newman suggests that what will ultimately transform our prayer life is recognizing what a privileged activity prayer is. Prayer is not simply an exalted form of conversation beyond what we experience with fellow human beings. It is quite literally intercourse with the world above. Through prayer, the Christian "pierces through the veil of this world and sees the next."[211] This activity is absolutely vital, because so often, as we

go about life, our vision is limited by what is most immediate to us — namely, the things and concerns of this world. Newman challenges his listeners to see beyond these realities, to address God "as a child might address his parent ... with [an] unmixed confidence in [God's provision]."[212] Approaching God in this way will help us to see this world for what it truly is — a gift, but also something that is temporary, which will one day make way for God's eternal kingdom.

Whenever Newman talks about "shadows and images" or about "piercing through the veil," he likely has in the back of his mind Plato's theory of the realm of forms, according to which the physical world participates in, or is rooted in, a more substantial reality (i.e., the world of forms). As an allegory to describe humanity's situation in the world, the great ancient philosopher used the illustration of a group of prisoners who find themselves chained inside a cave, with a fire nearby that casts shadows upon one of the walls of the cave. According to Plato's allegory, the prisoners are chained in such a way that only this wall is visible to them, and over time they come to believe that the shadows they see make up the whole of reality. By chance, one day a single prisoner gets free and, upon leaving the cave, discovers an expansive new world beyond his wildest imaginations.

This discovery, of course, is not pain-free. At first, the light from the sun is almost too much for the escapee to bear. But his eyes slowly adjust, and eventually he is able to see the world as it really is. Now Plato asks: What would it be like if this man returned to the cave and tried to explain to the other prisoners the reality of the outside world? They would likely think that he was crazy. And if he persisted in the face of their skepticism, they might even go so far as to harm him or try to eliminate him. Speaking the truth when others are not ready to hear it can be a dangerous venture indeed, as is evident from the examples of Socrates and Jesus.

Plato's allegory of the cave has been applied in a number of ways, but for our purposes, it could be seen to represent the prayerful believer. Those who have pierced the veil know that the world around us comprises shadows and images. In saying this, I don't have in mind so much the material world that God has created, but the world of politics, entertainment, and finance. Worldly persons treat those things as being all there is, but those with the gift of faith know that there is a much more substantial reality behind what is presently visible to us. The author of Hebrews touches on this same idea, when he makes reference to "a kingdom that cannot be shaken," elaborating that at a future date God will remove "what can be shaken — that is, created things — so that what cannot be shaken may remain" (Heb 12:27, NIV). Prayer, Newman indicates, has the power of giving us momentary glimpses into what is really real, or perhaps better, what is most real.

Newman also draws upon this set of ideas when he discusses Christ's Second Coming. In a challenging sermon titled "Worship, a Preparation for Christ's Coming," Newman contrasts our present experience of life in this world with what we will undergo when Our Lord returns in glory: "At present we are in a world of shadows," Newman observes. "What we see is not substantial. Suddenly it will be rent in twain and vanish away, and our Maker will appear. And then, I say, that first appearance will be nothing less than a personal intercourse between the Creator and every creature. He will look on us, while we look on Him."[213] Those who grasp what an awe-filled encounter awaits them will actively seek out ways of preparing for it. Newman places this topic of due preparation in the context of the liturgy, imagining an Advent scene in which early-morning worshippers brave a cold morning to visit their local church. His description of their motivation is instructive:

> The season is chill and dark, and the breath of
> the morning is damp, and worshippers are few,
> but all this befits those who are by profession
> penitents and mourners, watchers and pilgrims.

More dear to them that loneliness, more cheerful
that severity, and more bright that gloom, than all
those aids and appliances of luxury by which men
nowadays attempt to make prayer less disagree-
able to them. True faith does not covet comforts.
It only complains when it is forbidden to kneel. ...
Its only hardship is to be hindered, or to be ridi-
culed, when it would place itself as a sinner before
its Judge. They who realize that awful Day when
they shall see Him face to face, whose eyes are as
a flame of fire, will as little bargain to pray pleas-
antly now, as they will think of doing so then.[214]

At the end of this quote, Newman basically admonishes his
listeners to meditate on the four last things: death, judgment,
heaven, and hell. Those who cultivate an active awareness of the
reality of future judgment will not desire a life of luxury and ease
but will rejoice in hardships as a testing ground for their faith.

In another Advent sermon, Newman characterizes the outlook of the committed disciple as one of "watchfulness." The
command to be watchful recurs throughout the Gospels, as, for
instance, in Mark 13:35–37: "Watch ye therefore, for ye know
not when the Master of the house cometh; at even, or at mid-
night, or at the cock-crowing, or in the morning; lest coming
suddenly He find you sleeping. And what I say unto you, I say
unto all, *Watch*."[215] As motivation for heeding Christ's warning,
we have the example, Newman says, of Our Lord's first coming.
Even though several of the prophets had foretold the Messiah's
coming, and even though at that point in history the people of
Israel were waiting in eager expectation for the fulfillment of
God's promises, so many of them failed to recognize Christ's
coming. In fact, far more people missed the advent of the Messiah than recognized it. And some of those to whom the promises
had been given not only overlooked the Incarnation but, in fact,
turned against the Son of God. I think especially of King Herod,

who with maniacal zeal sought to hunt down and kill the new-born King. Newman sets this history before us as a warning. If the people of God were taken by surprise at Our Lord's first advent, the danger of being caught slumbering is even more acute with respect to the Second Coming, as in the latter instance he will return suddenly, "like a thief in the night" (1 Thes 5:2).

At the heart of the charge to remain watchful is prayerfulness. If we are going to raise our eyes above the shadows and illusions of earthly life, Newman says, we have to be consistently about the one activity that pierces the veil of this world and enables us to see what is truly lasting. And given just how essential prayer is to our remaining spiritually alert, we cannot afford to leave it up to the whims of our disposition, waiting for those occasions when we will feel inspired to speak with God. Rather, the seriousness of this task demands that we set aside fixed times for prayer. This is a difficult discipline to practice, and most of us, Newman conjectures, fail to achieve regularity in our prayer life:

> Most [Christians] indeed, I fear, neither pray at fixed times, nor do they cultivate an habitual communion with Almighty God. Indeed, it is too plain how most [persons] pray. They pray now and then, when they feel particular need of God's assistance; when they are in trouble or in apprehension of danger; or when their feelings are unusually excited. They do not know what it is either to be habitually religious, or to devote a certain number of minutes at fixed times to the thought of God. ... Let any man compare in his mind how many times he has prayed when in trouble, with how seldom he has returned thanks when his prayers have been granted; or the earnestness with which he prays against expected suffering, with the languor and unconcern of his thanksgivings afterwards, and he will soon see how little he

has of the real habit of prayer, and how much his religion depends on accidental excitement, which is no test of a religious heart. ... Why is this, except that his perception of the unseen world is not the true view which faith gives (else it would last as that world itself lasts), but a mere dream, which endures for a night, and is succeeded by a hard worldly joy in the morning?[216]

Newman's description of spiritual lethargy likely hits home for far too many of us. As we think about recalibrating our prayer life, we have no better example than Our Lord himself, who "often withdrew to deserted places and prayed" (Lk 5:16, NIV slightly altered). If the Son of God recognized the necessity and urgency of prayer, how much more should we be about the business of withdrawing from the busyness of life to spend time in the presence of our heavenly Father?

As a way of impressing upon his listeners just how vital prayer is to the spiritual life, Newman challenges them to keep ever before their eyes the reality that Christ will come again: "Year passes after year silently; Christ's coming is ever nearer than it was. O that, as He comes nearer earth, we may approach nearer heaven! O, my brethren, pray Him to give you the heart to seek Him in sincerity. Pray Him to make you in earnest."[217] This prayer — of a sincere desire to be with God — must be combined, Newman goes on to say, with humble cross-bearing: "You have one work only, to bear your cross after Him. Resolve in His strength to do so."[218] The world will try to knock us off course with both "promises and threats"; even some forms of religion — those that prize high professions or disputations over concrete action — can be a distraction to us.[219] "Without waiting," then, we need to "begin at once to obey Him" as best we know how, for as Newman notes: "Any obedience is better than none — any profession which is disjoined from obedience, is a mere pretense and deceit. Any religion which does not bring you nearer to God is of the world. You have to seek His face; [and] obedience is the only way of seeking Him."[220] As noted in an earlier chapter, Newman's spirituality is completely unsentimental: Deeds are always prioritized over lofty theological speech, no matter how sincere.

When discussing the importance of obedience, Newman once more returns to this idea of supernatural realities standing behind the veil of this visible world:

> Every act of obedience is an approach — an approach to Him who is not far off, though He seems so, but close behind this visible screen of things which hides Him from us. [God] is behind this material framework; earth and sky are but a veil going between Him and us; the day will come when He will rend that veil, and show Himself to us. And then, according as we have waited for Him, will He recompense us.[221]

The disciples in the Garden of Gethsemane did not intend to betray Jesus; they simply let their physical tiredness prevent them from keeping watch with their Lord. As to our situation, it may not be grave sins that trip us up. Very often, it's apathy or getting distracted by lesser goods that prevents us from doing the will of God. Prayer is one of the most effective means of waking us up from our spiritual slumber, because prayer immediately places us in the presence of Almighty God. Finally, when we pray, we ought to use the opportunity to reflect on the fact that one day we will have to stand before God and give an account of our lives. There may be no thought more likely to awake us from our slumber, Newman concludes, than to stop and evaluate one's life in light of eternity: "May this [i.e., Christ's finding us watchful] be the portion of every one of us! It is hard to attain it; but it is woeful to fail. Life is short; death is certain; and the world to come is everlasting."[222]

7

A GOOD DEATH

During the Middle Ages in the Christian West, those who designed churches would incorporate various artistic elements that were meant to remind churchgoers of death and final judgment. These reminders were a symbolic expression of the popular maxim *Memento mori*, roughly meaning "Remember that you must die." Whatever outcomes fortune may bring our way, one thing that each person knows for certain is that he must die. In the Christian imagination, the recognition of one's own mortality is supposed to have a sobering effect on how one approaches life. Whereas ancient pagans used to exclaim, "Eat, drink, and be merry, for tomorrow we die," serious Christians know that one day in the not-so-distant future they will be ushered into the presence of God and will have to give an account for all that they have done in the body. If what Christians confess is true, then every moment of every day is infused with eternal significance.

Newman lived his life under the banner of *Memento mori*. This was evident in his personal pursuit of holiness, but it also informed how he talked about the Faith with others. His sermons, for instance, regularly included reminders about the certainty of death and final judgment as a way of motivating his audience to live for God in the present. As a characteristic example, consider the following excerpt wherein Newman challenges his listeners to consider "what it is to die":

> Death puts an end absolutely and irrevocably to all our plans and works, and it is inevitable. ... Difficult as we may find it to bring it home to ourselves, to realize it, yet as surely as we are here assembled together, so surely will every one of us, sooner or later, one by one, be stretched on the bed of death. We naturally shrink from the thought of death, and of its attendant circumstances; but all that is hateful and fearful about it will be fulfilled in our case, one by one. But all this is nothing compared with the consequences implied in it. Death stops us; it stops our race. Men are engaged about their work, or about their pleasure; they are in the city, or the field; any how they are stopped; their deeds are suddenly gathered in — a reckoning is made — all is sealed up till the great day. What a change is this! In the words used familiarly in speaking of the dead, they are no more. They were full of schemes and projects; whether in a greater or humbler rank, they had their hopes and fears, their prospects, their pursuits, their rivalries; all these are now come to an end.[223]

The inevitability and finality of death ought to be a sobering thought, even for the young, yet for many of us it is not. As Newman says in the quote above, "We naturally shrink from the thought of death," while the dazzling sights of this world — the achievements and glories of human society — distract us from seeing what is eternal. The "sights of earth intoxicate," Newman writes elsewhere, "and its music is a spell upon the soul."[224] It takes real effort, in other words, to keep in view a lively sense of one's own mortality.

How differently we would go about our lives, Newman suggests, if we genuinely took to heart the "inevitable necessity" and "unspeakable importance" of death.[225] "Men on their death-beds have declared, that no one could form a right idea of the value of time till he came to die,"[226] yet how easy it is for those with good health or "in the prime of life" to squander away the time that is given to them. Newman recognizes that reflecting on one's own morality, while potentially serving as a spark of motivation, can also lead to feelings of discouragement, even dread, as the soul contemplates its sins and missed opportunities for repentance. Without mitigating the demands of the Gospel, Newman concludes this sermon with a reminder that we all "fall short of the glory of God" (Rom 3:23), and thus are all dependent on God's mercy:

> "Remember me, O Lord, when Thou comest into Thy kingdom." Such was the prayer of the penitent thief on the cross, such must be our prayer. Who can do us any good, but He, who shall also be our Judge? When shocking thoughts about ourselves come across us and afflict us, "Remember me," this is all we have to say. We have "no work, nor device, nor knowledge, nor wisdom" of our own, to better ourselves withal. We can say nothing to God in defense of ourselves — we can but acknowledge that we are grievous sinners, and addressing Him as suppliants, merely beg Him to bear us in mind in mercy, for His Son's sake to do us some favor, not according to our deserts, but for the love of Christ.[227]

When he turns to the topic of final judgment, then, Newman refuses to collapse the tension between divine and human freedom, and between the moral imperative and grace. It would be easy to fall back on the idea that "God does it all." But Newman, like Moses, boldly pronounces, "Choose you this day whom you will serve." Whenever he delivers such an admonition, however, it is almost always followed up by a reminder that apart from God's gracious assistance we would be helplessly lost in our sins. With exquisite rhetorical flair, the final paragraph of "The Lapse of Time" powerfully captures this tension inherent in the Christian life:

> Those whom Christ saves are they who at once attempt to save themselves, yet despair of saving themselves; who aim to do all, and confess they do naught; who are all love, and all fear; who are the most holy, and yet confess themselves the most sinful; who ever seek to please Him, yet feel they never can; who are full of good works, yet of works of penance. All this seems a contradiction to the natural man, but it is not so to those whom Christ enlightens. They understand in proportion to their illumination, that it is possible to work out their salvation, yet to have it wrought out for them, to fear and tremble at the thought of judgment, yet to rejoice always in the Lord, and hope and pray for His coming.[228]

Those who have placed their hope in Christ alone can pray with sincerity the terse prayer given to us by Saint Paul, *Marana-tha* — "Our Lord, come!" (1 Cor 16:22).

GOD'S WILL AND THE END OF LIFE

One of the major challenges, it seems, in our preparation for death is that the wonder and glamour of this world lull us into thinking that the world can "supply all that we need."[229] If we are not careful, we are likely to get carried away by the spectacle of human society, which deceptively conveys the impression of being able to satisfy our every desire:

> Go abroad into the streets of the populous city, contemplate the continuous outpouring there of human energy, and the countless varieties of human character, and be satisfied! The ways are thronged, carriage-way and pavement; multitudes are hurrying to and fro, each on his own errand, or are loitering about from listlessness, or from want of work, or have come forth into the public concourse, to see and to be seen, for amusement or for display, or on the excuse of business. The carriages of the wealthy mingle with the slow wains laden with provisions or merchandise, the productions of art or the demands of luxury. The streets are lined with shops, open and gay, inviting customers, and widen now and then into some spacious square or place, with lofty masses of brickwork or of stone, gleaming in the fitful sunbeam, and surrounded or fronted with what simulates a garden's foliage. Follow them in another direction, and you find the whole groundstead covered with large buildings, planted thickly up and down, the homes of the mechanical arts. The air is filled, below, with a ceaseless, importunate, monotonous din, which penetrates even to your most innermost chamber, and rings in your ears even when you are not conscious of it; and overhead, with a canopy of smoke, shrouding God's day from the realms of obstinate sullen toil. This is the end of man![230]

Newman's evocative language in this passage calls to mind the experience of walking down a busy city street — say, in Paris or New York. On such occasions, it's easy to fall into the mindset of thinking that what lies before one's eyes will last forever. The hustle and bustle of a modern downtown have a mesmerizing quality and can cause us to forget that one day all of this will be swept away.

To avoid falling into this trap, we have to begin to see the world as God sees it.[231] We must aim, in other words, to view the surface realities of life in this world through the lens of deeper, spiritual truths. This is no easy task, Newman admits. Take, for instance, the Church's teaching that at death the soul is separated from the body. "Nothing is more difficult," Newman writes, "than to realize that every [person] has a distinct soul, that every one of all the millions who live or have lived, is as whole and independent a being in himself as if there were no one else in the whole world but he."[232] At first glance, it might appear that Newman is advancing a radical individualism in this sermon, but he is actually trying to impress upon his readers the inherent dignity and value of each individual. When we survey the "splendor, magnificence, opulence, and energy" of "some populous town," we can forget that the crowd pouring through the streets does not comprise an undifferentiated multitude, but is in reality "a collection of immortal souls."[233] This insight impacts also how we look back at the details of history: We tend to speak of "multitudes," but what preceded us, properly speaking, was a vast chain of individual persons. Each one of those persons "not only had while he was upon earth, but *has* a soul, which did in its own time but return to God who gave it, and not perish, and which now lives unto Him. All those millions upon millions of human beings who ever trod the earth and saw the sun successively, are at this very moment in existence all together."[234]

Recognizing the immortality of the soul has two payoffs. As to our personal responsibility before God, it is one of the most potent ways of focusing our attention on what really matters. In

Newman's words, "To discern our immortality is necessarily connected with fear and trembling and repentance."[235] The one who was granted even a momentary glimpse of hell "would be henceforth dead to the pleasures and employments of this world, considered in themselves, thinking of them only in their reference to that fearful vision."[236] The affairs of life, however, have a way of drawing our attention away from enduring realities and of obscuring the certainty of final judgment. As in the movie *The Matrix* or Plato's allegory of the cave, the surface-level matters of life tend to monopolize our vision, distracting us from what is "most really real." Taking time to reflect upon the four last things — death, judgment, heaven, and hell — can help to awaken us from our slumber and prepare us to respond to God's call. As Newman summarizes the matter, those who are "absorbed in the thought of the life to come are [the ones] who really and heartily receive the words of Christ and His Apostles."[237]

As to our relationships with others, Newman suggests that recognizing the spiritual dimension of each person will fundamentally transform how we view the moral life. "No thought ... is more overpowering," he writes, "than that every one who lives or has lived is destined for endless bliss or torment."[238] To put it in other terms, each soul is "in one of two spiritual states": either "on the way to eternal happiness" or on the path "to eternal misery."[239] Until the moment of death, the gulf that separates a person from God is "not impassable."[240] As long as we have breath, then, we should be about redeeming the time (see Eph 5:16) — avoiding sin while doing as much as possible to assist others along the way toward God. Newman continues: "How blessed would it be, if we really understood this! What a change it would produce in our thoughts ... to understand what and where we are — accountable beings on their trial, with God for their friend and the devil for their enemy, and advanced a certain way on their road either to heaven or to hell."[241] These truths are not idle speculations. They have real-life consequences. As we learn to see reality through the eyes of faith, we will increasingly recognize that this life is not about pursuing personal gain or temporary pleasures. Rather, as Newman highlights, it is a kind of testing ground, an opportunity to purge ourselves of sinful desires so that we will be prepared for eternal communion with God. Furthermore, our destiny is always caught up with the destiny of others, for in the economy of grace, God deigns to use the company of the redeemed to draw others into the kingdom of heaven.

C. S. Lewis offers a similar vision of human relations in a widely read essay called "The Weight of Glory." There, Lewis asserts that we should always aim to see our neighbor with an eye to that person's eternal destiny. Lewis describes our neighbor's potential glory as a "load," or "weight," which we should seek daily to carry upon our backs. As he memorably puts it:

> It is a serious thing to live in a society of possible
> gods and goddesses, to remember that the dullest
> and most uninteresting person you talk to may
> one day be a creature which, if you saw it now,
> you would be strongly tempted to worship, or
> else a horror and a corruption such as you now
> meet, if at all, only in a nightmare. All day long
> we are, in some degree, helping each other to one
> or other of these destinations. It is in the light of
> these overwhelming possibilities, it is with the
> awe and the circumspection proper to them, that
> we should conduct all our dealings with one an-
> other, all friendships, all loves, all play, all politics.
> There are no *ordinary* people.[242]

Like Newman, Lewis believes that a serious consideration of the reality that each person has been created to live eternally will transform our everyday relations with our neighbor. Lewis concludes profoundly, "Next to the Blessed Sacrament itself, your neighbor is the holiest object presented to your senses. If he is your Christian neighbor he is holy in almost the same way, for in him also Christ *vere latitat* — the glorifier and the glorified, Glory Himself, is truly hidden."[243] Given the seriousness of what's at stake, we should ask God for the grace "to look at things as God looks at them, and judge of them as He judges."[244] With God's vision of the world, we will begin to see all of our encounters with other persons for what they really are: moments bearing the weight of eternity, in which we have the opportunity, by our actions, either to draw others closer to, or push them away from, the presence of God.

THE VALUE OF A SINGLE SOUL

Here's the bottom line: Your soul is of inestimable value. "What does it profit a person," Our Lord says, "if he gains the whole world, yet loses his soul?" (Mk 8:36, slightly altered). There is nothing, in other words, that's worth obtaining in exchange for one's own soul. As we go about life, however, it's all too easy to lose sight of that reality. The world presents a dizzying array of sights and sounds — distractions, really — that can deceive us into thinking that what surrounds us is permanent and worth clinging to. Newman was attentive to the way that the world could distract Christians from core realities. In one reflection on God's will being "the end of life," he starkly lays out just how much of a distraction the world can be: "The world professes to supply all that we need, as if we were sent into it for the sake of being sent here, and for nothing beyond the sending. ... Every man is doing his own will here, seeking his own pleasure, pursuing his own ends, and that [appears to be] why he was brought into existence."[245] Recall, Newman penned this passage long prior to the advent of electronic technologies and social media. In our own day, it is arguably even more difficult to avoid becoming enamored with the enticements of this world, and thus we ought to redouble our petitions for the grace to live with detachment.

All that being said, the world — in and of itself — is not the problem. From Newman's vantage point, Christians are called not to reject the world but to view it in light of eternity. In an apt little phrase, Newman describes the "world of sense" as a "veil," or "curtain," meaning that it can serve as an opening to an even more expansive reality.[246] In his *Apologia Pro Vita Sua*, Newman expands upon this point by referring to the "sacramental principle," which is a term he uses to describe the way in which the physical world points beyond itself to a greater reality. In Newman's words, "I understood these passages [from the Church Fathers] to mean that the exterior world, physical and historical, was but the manifestation to our senses of realities greater than itself. Nature was a parable: Scripture was an allegory: pagan literature, philosophy, and mythology, properly understood, were but a preparation for the Gospel."[247] The "divine economy," or way in which God works, is not through revealing to us secret knowledge or even, necessarily, by wowing us with some sort of miraculous interruption into our normal affairs. Rather, God uses the things of this world — water, bread, wine, oil, salt, and so forth — to open our eyes to his presence and to impart to us supernatural grace.

So the question becomes: How do we go about receiving the things of this world as channels of God's grace while avoiding the temptation to "fix our minds on things below"? How, in other words, do we learn to treat the world as a veil and not as our permanent home? For Newman, the answer is simple: we have to begin to cultivate an awareness of the fact that we are eternal beings. Even though life after death is a doctrine of the Christian faith, too many of us walk around without a clear sense of what this truth entails. It constitutes head knowledge for us but has no real impact on our lived existence. Newman writes:

> And yet, in spite of our being able to speak about [the immortality of the soul] and our "form of knowledge" ... there seems scarcely room to doubt, that the greater number of those who are

called Christians in no true sense realize it in their own minds at all. Indeed, it is a very difficult thing to bring home to us, and to feel, that we have souls; and there cannot be a more fatal mistake than to suppose we see what the doctrine means, as soon as we can use the words which signify it. So great a thing is it to understand that we have souls, that the knowing it, taken in connection with its results, is all one with being serious, i.e., truly religious. To discern our immortality is necessarily connected with fear and trembling and repentance, in the case of every Christian. Who is there but would be sobered by an actual sight of the flames of hell fire and the souls therein hopelessly enclosed? Would not all his thoughts be drawn to that awful sight, so that he would stand still gazing fixedly upon it, and forgetting everything else; seeing nothing else, hearing nothing, engrossed with the contemplation of it; and when the sight was withdrawn, still having it fixed in his memory, so that he would be henceforth dead to the pleasures and employments of this world, considered in themselves, thinking of them only in their reference to that fearful vision?[248]

On one level, Newman's rhetoric in this excerpt could be described, disparagingly, as an example of "fire and brimstone" preaching, a style of preaching in which the homilist tries to frighten his listeners into repentance. But, if one balances this passage with the vast corpus of Newman's sermons, one will find that, for Newman, the central motivating factor in the struggle for holiness is not fear but the prospect of attaining union with an all-loving God. Nevertheless, the inverse reality cannot be ignored. Hell names the state of those who refuse that union, in effect saying to God, "Not thy will, but mine be done." As with

Satan in Milton's famous poem, the impenitent would rather rule (themselves) in hell than serve God in heaven. Those who definitively refuse the free gift of grace do not fall outside the orbit of God's love; however, they experience that love as wrath instead of beatitude.

Newman, from a young age, seemed to possess a special aptitude for seeing himself in relation to God. In his autobiography, he reports that, ever since childhood, he had felt a certain "[isolation] from the objects which surrounded me ... confirming me in my mistrust of the reality of material phenomena, and making me rest in the thought of two and two only absolute and luminously self-evident beings, myself and my Creator."[249] Within the tradition of Christian spirituality, there have historically been two poles with respect to conceptualizing salvation. On one side, certain writers have emphasized the communion of saints, or network of the faithful (both living and dead), who are seen to be journeying together toward a common home.[250] According to this outlook, no person is an island, and our eternal destiny is always necessarily caught up in God's plan for redeeming an entire people and, in fact, the whole of creation. Without rejecting the insights of this first approach, other spiritual writers have tended to highlight our individual standing before God. The call to repentance reaches each one of us as particular persons, and every individual bears a personal responsibility to heed that call. Though the moral life by its very nature has a communal character, strictly speaking, each one of us will have to answer for how we responded to the Gospel and what we did with the time allotted to us.

In my estimation, Newman leans strongly in the direction of the latter approach. There are numerous places in his sermons, of course, where he highlights the individual Christian's relation to and reliance upon the corporate Body of Christ. But, fundamentally, he presses his listeners to consider, as individuals, their personal standing before Almighty God. As he puts it in one sermon, "To every one of us there are but two beings in the whole world, himself and God; for as to this outward scene, its pleasures and pursuits, its honors and cares, its contrivances, its personages, its kingdoms, its multitude of busy slaves, what are they to us? Nothing — no more than a show: — 'The world passeth away and the lust thereof.' "[251] There is something convicting, Newman intimates, about meditating upon the immortality of the soul: to consider, really consider, that we *will* live forever, that the things of this world are passing away, and that at some point each one of us will have to give an account of our actions performed in this world.

Regularly calling to mind our eternal destiny and the prospect of final judgment, when done in cooperation with divine grace, will help us to foster a healthy detachment from wealth, relationships, and other temporal goods. The good things of this world — food, clothing, relaxation, and so forth — are, most certainly, gifts from God and not to be shunned as things that are intrinsically bad. But it is easy, Newman warns, for us to elevate these goods above where they belong, such that they begin to crowd God out of our lives. On this point, Newman is stricter than many standard preachers. We have to be on guard, he cautions, not simply against temptation to serious sin, but also against spiritual complacency, against *acedia*, or what he sometimes describes as softness. In his view, "Nothing is so likely to corrupt our hearts, and to seduce us from God, as to surround ourselves with comforts — to have things our own way."[252] A person in this state comes to see himself as the center of the world and over time develops the habit of seeing his possessions as necessary to his well-being, rather than as gifts to be shared. If his wealth and status happen to be taken away from him, he will descend into a state of despair, because he had placed his trust in material things and not in God. In contrast, "to understand that we have souls, is to feel our separation from things visible, our independence of them ... our power of acting for ourselves in this way or that way, our accountableness for what we do."[253] Let us ask God to grant us the grace of this understanding.

GOD'S STRANGE PROVIDENCE

In his own life, Newman learned to trust in God by undergoing various trials. One of the most significant events in his spiritual journey was his experience of a serious illness (probably typhoid fever), which he contracted while on a trip to Sicily in 1833.[254] Looking back on this event, Newman interpreted the illness as a chastisement sent by God, meant to temper his willfulness. The trip to Sicily during which Newman became sick had not originally been part of his plans. He started the trip with his best friend, Hurrell Froude, and Froude's father, Robert. However, after visiting both Sicily and Rome — as they planned — Newman made a spur-of-the-moment decision to return to Sicily rather than traveling back to England with his companions. In retrospect, Newman saw this decision as a sign of willfulness on his part, something he had condemned during a sermon he preached (ironically) on the very day before he left on the trip.[255]

Cognizant of his stubbornness, Newman now believed that the illness was sent by God to chasten his self-will. "The Lord disciplines those whom he loves" (Heb 12:6, NRSV), the author of Hebrews tells us, and this was certainly true of Newman's life. In this case, Newman could be grateful for having been "laid low," however difficult the experience may have been at the time. The "strange providence"[256] that Newman perceived in these events served as the inspiration for one of his most famous works of poetry, "The Pillar of the Cloud," best known for the verse that after his death became a popular piece of hymnody:

> Lead, Kindly Light, amid the encircling gloom
>   Lead Thou me on!
> The night is dark, and I am far from home —
>   Lead Thou me on!
> Keep Thou my feet; I do not ask to see
> The distant scene — one step enough for me.[257]

The final phrase of this stanza ("one step enough for me") brings into relief a temptation that besets many of us — namely, the desire to see beyond the present in order to know what the future holds. Considering our status as children of God, however, we ought to live in the trust that God will watch over us today and provide for us in the future. In the normal order of things, children do not chart the course of their lives but remain dependent on their parents, who know far more about the ways of the world and about what will contribute best to their children's flourishing. How much more are we dependent on our heavenly Father for life and well-being?

Dwelling excessively on the future is a sign of distrust, because it indicates that we wish to manage circumstances that are beyond our control. In doing so, we fall into the same trap that our first parents did, aspiring to be like God rather than humbly accepting our creaturely status. When faced with this temptation, we ought to call to mind the admonition of Jesus: "Therefore do not be anxious about tomorrow, for tomorrow will be anxious for itself. Let the day's own trouble be sufficient for the day" (Mt 6:34). One way we can begin to build our trust in God's care is simply by reciting Newman's prayer in the poem cited above: "Lead, Kindly Light, lead Thou me on ... I do not ask to see the distant scene — one step enough for me." As we lean more and more upon God, this renewed sense of trust will transform how we think about temporal goods. Even though the world "professes to supply all that we need," at some point the disappointments of life will expose "the vanity and unprofitableness" of all that it has to offer.[258] As Newman highlights, God alone is "the stay of the soul."[259]

Newman was blessed with the grace of recognizing this fact at a young age. Since he did not view this world as his home, he did not expect God, necessarily, to lavish him with worldly goods or to help him reach any temporal achievement. Detachment from such things was crucial to Newman's understanding of what it means to abandon oneself to divine providence. Newman lays all of this out in a moving prayer in his *Meditations and Devotions*:

> God has created me to do Him some definite ser-
> vice; He has committed some work to me which
> He has not committed to another. I have my mis-
> sion — I never may know it in this life, but I shall
> be told it in the next. Somehow I am necessary
> for His purposes, as necessary in my place as an
> Archangel in his — if, indeed, I fail, He can raise
> another, as He could make the stones children of
> Abraham. Yet I have a part in this great work; I
> am a link in a chain, a bond of connection be-
> tween persons. He has not created me for naught.
> I shall do good, I shall do His work; I shall be an
> angel of peace, a preacher of truth in my own
> place, while not intending it, if I do but keep His
> commandments and serve Him in my calling.
> Therefore I will trust Him. Whatever, wher-
> ever I am, I can never be thrown away. If I am
> in sickness, my sickness may serve Him; in per-
> plexity, my perplexity may serve Him; if I am in
> sorrow, my sorrow may serve Him. My sickness,
> or perplexity, or sorrow may be necessary caus-
> es of some great end, which is quite beyond us.
> He does nothing in vain; He may prolong my life,
> He may shorten it; He knows what He is about.
> He may take away my friends, He may throw me
> among strangers, He may make me feel desolate,
> make my spirits sink, hide the future from me—
> still He knows what He is about.[260]

As is evident from this prayer, Newman trusted (a) that God had a specific mission for him to accomplish and (b) that God would sustain him until that mission was complete. Thus, Newman did not feel any anxiety about the circumstances of his life — whether he would face sickness or lose friends or even that his life might be unusually short. His highest concern, above any other consideration, was to serve God by keeping God's commandments.

The recognition that heaven was his home did not mean, for Newman, that this world is without value or is to be neglected. To the contrary, seen in the light of eternity, each moment of life is infinitely valuable, for it is on earth — in the time and place that God has ordained for us — that we work out our salvation, attaining "to the measure of the stature of the fulness of Christ " (Eph 4:13). "The one great rule," as Newman deemed it, of God's dealings with humanity is "that the visible world is the instrument, yet the veil, of the world invisible — the veil, yet still partially the symbol and index: so that all that exists or happens visibly, conceals and yet suggests, and above all subserves, a system of persons, facts, and events beyond itself."[261] Unlike some worldviews that posit a sharp dichotomy between this world and the next, Christianity sees this world both as good and as disclosing the reality of a higher world. "All that is seen" and all that we experience — if viewed through the eyes of faith — can disclose the wonderful plan of God and the nature of ultimate reality.[262] This world cannot be cast aside or devalued, because it is through it that we come to know God.

We see this truth confirmed in the ways that God has chosen to draw us into the divine life. Immersion in water becomes a means of supernatural birth. Bread and wine, when consecrated, convey the presence of God. Pain and loss need not be meaningless but become opportunities to unite our suffering with Christ's Passion, so that by being "united with him in a death like his, we will certainly also be united with him in a resurrection like his" (Rom 6:5). And thus, even death is transformed: rather than being an event that circumscribes our life, and brings an end to our dreams, it becomes a passageway into a new and greater life.

THE DREAM OF GERONTIUS

This hope of being raised to new life in Christ was central to Newman's overall outlook. If God is faithful in guiding us through the vicissitudes of life, he will certainly not abandon us at the point of death. Newman touches on the theme of a good death in a number of places in his writings, but his most extended reflection on that topic is *The Dream of Gerontius*, a poem that he composed in 1865 and that grew in popularity after the composer Edward Elgar set it to music in 1900. *The Dream* dramatically narrates the final moments of the life of an elderly man, Gerontius, as he crosses the threshold between this world and the next. Gerontius, whose name simply means "old man," represents all pious believers, who, though we have been redeemed by Christ, must still suffer natural death as a result of our sins. Over the course of the poem, the reader learns scant details about Gerontius's life. This characteristic of the poem serves an important function. By telling of Gerontius's death in this manner, Newman depicts the "passage" that every soul must take "from this life to eternity" and thereby invites each of us to take stock of our own mortality.[263]

In his commentary on *The Dream*, Roderick Strange notes that Gerontius is "a good man but not a saint." He "has been saved," for sure, and "will go to heaven; but first he must be purified."[264] On his deathbed, Gerontius is surrounded by loved ones who offer various prayers from the Roman Ritual while pleading with Our Lady and the saints to intercede on behalf of their dying friend. The prayerful support of these friends is vital to Gerontius, for it is the only thing preventing him from being overwhelmed by what is now taking place within him.

Now that he finds himself at death's door, "no room is left for self-deception."[265] Gerontius sees unmistakably that his life is ending and, faced with this prospect, sees that the only sensible action left to take is to beg God for mercy:

> Jesu, Maria — I am near to death,
> And Thou art calling me; I know it now.
> Not by the token of this faltering breath,
> This chill at heart, this dampness on my brow
> —
>
> (Jesu, have mercy! Mary, pray for me!)
> 'Tis this new feeling, never felt before,
> (Be with me, Lord, in my extremity!)
> That I am going, that I am no more.[266]

Over the course of the next several stanzas, Newman compellingly depicts the fear that most of us will have to face down when we reach the final hours of our earthly lives, if we are spared a sudden death. Gerontius laments the "emptying out of each constituent and natural force" in his body, but more difficult still is the "strange innermost abandonment" that he feels in his soul.[267] Death appears to Gerontius quite like a demon, "knocking his dire summons at my door, the like of whom, to scare me and to daunt, has never, never come to me before."[268]

Newman's depiction of the psychological trials that normally accompany death is, in a word, harrowing. At one point in the poem, Gerontius confesses that this facet of his experience is more intense than the physical pain involved:

> I can no more; for now it comes again,
> That sense of ruin, which is worse than pain,
> That masterful negation and collapse
> Of all that makes me man; as though I bent
> Over the dizzy brink
> Of some sheer infinite descent.[269]

Feeling as if he is falling through the order of created things into some "vast abyss," Gerontius cries out that "a fierce and restless fright begins to fill the mansion of my soul."[270] Although beset by fear, he does not succumb to despair. While pleading with his friends for their continued aid ("Pray for me, O my friends ... "), Gerontius garners the strength to make a moving expression of faith, both confessing his belief in what God has revealed — "Firmly I believe and truly, God is Three, and God is One" etc. — and also humbly accepting "*with joy*" whatever "pain or fear" shall accompany his dying.[271]

In the judgment of writer John Cornwell, it is at the moment of Gerontius's death that "the verse begins to attain imaginative power."[272] Gerontius describes his death as a kind of sleep, and upon waking, "a strange refreshment" and "inexpressive light-ness" pervades him. The power of Newman's rhetoric imagina-tively draws the reader into something of what it must be like to pass into that higher realm:

> This silence pours a solitariness
> Into the very essence of my soul;
> And the deep rest, so soothing and so sweet,
> Hath something too of sternness and of pain.[273]

But Gerontius's journey is not yet over. In this liminal place, Gerontius's guardian angel comes to greet him, and, while the angel's "work is done" and Gerontius's salvation is assured ("For the crown is won"), the recently deceased must undergo a pur-gative process before he is adequately prepared for eternal com-munion with his Creator and Lord.[274]

Over the years, the devotional life connected to the doctrine of purgatory has taken on different tones, or emphases. In cer-tain eras, the prospect of experiencing purgatory was viewed mostly with trepidation by the faithful: the focus was on the pain that would accompany the purgative process, and the faith-ful were counseled to do all they could to avoid this destination. Without dismissing out of hand this element of the devotional tradition, Newman's accent falls in a different place. Purgatory, as Newman depicts it, is one way of naming what the imper-fect soul goes through when it is ushered into the presence of

God. Because Gerontius had a proper fear of God while alive, he now has no fear of meeting his Divine Judge but approaches the throne of God "with a serenest joy." Paradoxically, this is a "happy, suffering soul" — "for it is safe, consumed, yet quicken'd, by the glance of God."[275] The "flame of the Everlasting Love" scorches Gerontius, yet he welcomes its embrace, for he knows that it is the very means by which God is bringing to completion the purification that began at his baptism.

When the purgative process commences, then, Gerontius expresses not fear but peace, commenting that "a deep mysterious harmony" now floods his spirit, "like the deep and solemn sound of many waters."[276] As the poem nears its dénouement, Gerontius's guardian angel passes his charge off to the "Angels of Purgatory," much as a caring physician might transfer a patient in her care to another medical team:

> And ye, great powers,
> Angels of Purgatory, receive from me
> My charge, a precious soul, until the day,
> When, from all bond and forfeiture released,
> I shall reclaim it for the courts of light.[277]

At this point, Gerontius is enveloped in the songs of the other souls in purgatory, who praise God for his justice as they await their release. And then, in the final stanza of the poem, the perspective again shifts back to that of the guardian angel, who sings a final word over Gerontius, soothingly reminiscent of a lullaby:

> Softly and gently, dearly-ransom'd soul,
>   In my most loving arms I now enfold thee,
>   And, o'er the penal waters, as they roll,
>   I poise thee, and I lower thee, and hold thee.[278]

This is a "farewell," the angel admits, but not one that shall last forever. The night of trial will pass swiftly, and, in the meantime, Gerontius will be aided by "Masses on the earth, and prayers in heaven."[279]

Newman's poem has an impressive pastoral quality to it, in that readers who immerse themselves in the text are led on an imaginative preview of the experience of death. Newman is starkly honest about the pain and the fear that normally accompany this most significant of points in a person's existence. But he also brings into sharp relief the reasons why Christians should approach the prospect of death with hope and even "with the serenest of joy," confident that their ultimate destiny is secure in the loving promises of God.

The doctrine of purgatory, moreover, ought to be for Christians a source of consolation, not anxiety. Yes, we have strong motivations for doing penance now, while on earth. We also know that, even though our penances are imperfect, God will not leave unfinished the work that he began in us. Purgatory is, in a certain light, the final act of purification that divine love performs on a person. After an individual is exposed to the purgative "flame of Eternal love," there will no longer be any obstacles that stand in the way of that person's being fully pervaded by the light of God's presence.

Certain characteristics of Newman's vision of purgatory anticipated ways that more recent theologians have begun to think about purgatory. Rather than conceptualizing purgatory according to measures of time, Newman highlights that we cannot presently grasp what duration will entail in that state of existence: "in the immaterial world ... time is not a common property," but "intervals in their succession are measured by the living thought alone."[280] Additionally, Newman depicts purgatory not so much as a place to which one is sent, but more so as the experience that one undergoes upon encountering the fullness of God's presence in the moments after death. Thinking about purgatory in these terms casts a new light, as well, on the traditional imagery of the fires of purgatory. In his encyclical letter

Spe Salvi, Pope Benedict XVI elaborates on this point:

> Some recent theologians are of the opinion that
> the fire which both burns and saves is Christ
> himself, the Judge and Savior. The encounter
> with him is the decisive act of judgement. Before
> his gaze all falsehood melts away. This encounter
> with him, as it burns us, transforms and frees us,
> allowing us to become truly ourselves. All that we
> build during our lives can prove to be mere straw,
> pure bluster, and it collapses. Yet in the pain of
> this encounter, when the impurity and sickness
> of our lives become evident to us, there lies sal-
> vation. His gaze, the touch of his heart heals us
> through an undeniably painful transformation
> "as through fire" [1 Cor 3:15]. But it is a blessed
> pain, in which the holy power of his love sears
> through us like a flame, enabling us to become
> totally ourselves and thus totally of God.[281]

The final sentences of this quotation really get at the heart
of the matter: However we end up conceptualizing the pain of
purgatory, we should keep in view that it will be for our good
and not for our ruin. The fire of purgatory, properly understood,
is not a punishing flame but one fueled by love. For those of us
who are not prepared at the point of death to enter heaven, this
flame will be the source of transformation — "enabling us to become totally ourselves," freed from all self-deception and therefore able to rest eternally in God's loving embrace.

EPILOGUE

LOVE, THE SEED OF HOLINESS

For the past several months, I have been teaching a tenth-grade catechetical course at my church. Whenever we wade through some particularly difficult material, I try to bring the conversation back to the basics. With Catholic theology, there can be a lot to think about: transubstantiation, indulgences, the Immaculate Conception, the two natures of Christ — the list goes on. It's not as though any one of these doctrines is insignificant; nevertheless, we should take time regularly to pause and recall what lies at the heart of our faith: "Beloved, let us love one another; for love is of God, and he who loves is born of God and knows God. He who does not love does not know God; for God is love. In this the love of God was made manifest among us, that God sent his only Son into the world, so that we might live through him" (1 Jn 4:7–8). God is love; God wants us to know his love; being a member of the Body of Christ is fundamentally about experiencing the fullness of God's love and then sharing that love with others.

Over the course of his life, Saint John Henry Newman wrote several highly intellectual essays, but he also had a knack, especially in his preaching, for bringing his audience's attention back to the heart of matters. In one sermon in which he unpacks the differences between faith and love, Newman reminds us that "love ... is the seed of holiness."[282] It does not get much more basic than that. Throughout this book, we have explored the topic of holiness from different angles, and in a longer book, other avenues could be pursued as well. At a very basic level, however, holiness has to do simply with allowing God's love to take full bloom in every facet of one's life. We should be careful never to lose sight of that foundational truth.

So, what does it look like to allow God's love to permeate our existence? In the sermon just quoted, Newman frames the matter this way: "Love is the gentle, tranquil, satisfied acquiescence and adherence of the soul in the contemplation of God; not only a preference of God before all things, but a delight in Him because He is God, and because His commandments are good."[283] The vision that Newman casts in this sermon really gets at the essence of love. What does it mean to love? It is not simply to prefer God to other things; it is to delight in God, precisely because God is our highest good. This insight casts a fresh light, as well, on how we view God's commandments. As Newman points out, because God is the good that he wills, God's commandments are good, and they exist for our own good. We are not slaves who are subservient to a fickle master but are children of a heavenly Father, who desires for us to be happy. God's commands, rather than being burdens that we have to grin and bear, are the very means by which we attain the happiness that he intends for us.

Love, then, leads to obedience — or, perhaps better stated,

love is made manifest in obedience to God's will. Our Lord himself highlights this point while teaching his disciples about the sending of the Holy Spirit: "Anyone who loves me will obey my teaching. My Father will love them, and we will come to them and make our home with them" (Jn 14:23, NIV). Again, approaching obedience in these terms changes the way we normally think about following commands. God's commandments are not arbitrary rules externally imposed to curtail our enjoyment of life, but are divinely ordained in order for us to experience God's love and then return that love to God. Jesus not only connects obedience to love, but he also indicates the divinely provided source by which we are enabled to love: "If you love me, you will keep my commandments. And I will ask the Father, and he will give you another Counselor, to be with you for ever, even the Spirit of truth" (Jn 14:15–17). In other words, as we saw in chapter 4, we are able to love as God loves because God makes his dwelling within us (see Rom 5:5). "The great promise of the Gospel," as Newman says, is "that the Lord of all, who had hitherto manifested Himself externally to His servants, should take up His abode in their hearts."[284]

As God's love expands in our hearts, we will feel less and less at home in this world. Newman captures this characteristic of the Christian life under the umbrella term of "watchfulness." The obedient Christian is a watchful person — someone who is "detached from what is present" and who "live[s] in what is unseen."[285] One of the surest indicators, then, of whether we are growing in faith is how at home we feel in the world. Do we look forward in eager anticipation to Christ's Second Coming, or do we live in anxiety of losing our possessions and our status? "This is the very definition of a Christian," Newman writes, "one who looks for Christ; not who looks for gain, or distinction, or power, or pleasure, or comfort, but who looks 'for the Savior, the Lord Jesus Christ.' This, according to Scripture, is the essential mark, this is the foundation of a Christian, from which everything else follows."[286] The Bible makes clear that this world is not our home

(Heb 13:14). The watchful Christian does not simply give lip service to this idea but lives in the reality of it.

Newman ties all of these ideas together in a remarkable sermon in which he describes "the essence of true conversion [as] unconditional surrender" to God.[287] Surrender, Newman goes on to say, is having a "perfect heart," not being "double-minded," but loving God with "sincerity" and "simplicity."[288] Building on these ideas, Newman pleads with his listeners:

> Since this is our privilege [i.e., to be justified by grace through faith] ... let us endeavor to become friends of God and fellow-citizens with the saints; not by sinless purity, for we have it not; not in our deeds of price, for we have none to show; not in our privileges, for they are God's acts, not ours; not in our Baptism, for it is outward; but in that which is the fruit of Baptism within us, not a word but a power, not a name but a reality, which, though it can claim nothing, can beg everything — an honest purpose, an unreserved, entire submission of ourselves to our Maker, Redeemer, and Judge. Let us beg Him to aid us in our endeavor, and, as He has begun a good work in us, to perform it until the day of the Lord Jesus.[289]

For Newman, this ultimately is what the life of grace looks like: friendship with God, communion with the saints, and complete submission to the divine will. As Newman observes, the total surrender of self to which the Gospel calls us is "a saying which most [persons] cannot receive."[290] Most of us "wish to be saved, but in [our] own way; [we] wish (as it were) to capitulate upon terms, to carry off [our] goods with [us]."[291] However, there is no approaching God apart from total surrender, that is to say, with absolute abandon: "The kingdom of heaven is like treasure hidden in a field, which a man found and covered up;

then in his joy he goes *and sells all that he has* and buys that field"
(Mt 13:44, emphasis added). Anyone with ears to hear should
listen and understand!

RUNNING WITH ENDURANCE

One paradoxical characteristic of human existence is that
time passes by very quickly — as is commonly said, time flies
— yet the journey of faith often feels more like a marathon
than a sprint. That is precisely why we tend to describe faith
as a "journey": the destination is not reached in a day, but for
most of us, it involves decades of arduous struggle. Newman
concurs. True conversion of heart, he says, "is not done in a
moment — it is a slow work."[292] Though sudden conversions
do happen, they are not the norm, and even these have to be
nourished over the long haul if they are to bear lasting fruit.
The vast majority of us stumble at different points along the
way and have to pick ourselves up again. "It is a great and arduous thing to attain to heaven," Newman notes, and we will
need to run with endurance in order to reach the finish line
(see Heb 12:1–2).

The race metaphor is an apt one, but we could also think
about the Christian life as a long journey across uncharted ter-
ritory — something like the epic adventure that J. R. R. Tolkien
depicts in his classic fantasy trilogy *The Lord of the Rings.* If you
have ever been on a multiday hike, you know that one temptation can be to turn back when the going gets tough. On such
occasions, our surroundings can also be a source of temptation.
Perhaps along the way you pass a town with a comfortable-look-
ing inn. To stop might serve as a source of relief for your aching
feet, but if the inn is too comfortable, you very likely could end
up staying longer than you intended or even give up on the journey altogether.

In the circumstances of life, this latter temptation mani-
fests itself in different ways — whether through the comforts of
home, through relationships, or through personal tastes. Aware

of these factors, Newman, in a sermon, spurs on his fellow so-journers: "Let us not be content with ourselves; let us not make our own hearts our home, or this world our home, or our friends our home; let us look out for a better country, that is, a heavenly [one]. ... Let us call heaven our home, and this life a pilgrimage."[293] In the same sermon, Newman basically echoes a charge given in the book of Hebrews. The author of Hebrews counsels us to "fix our eyes on Jesus, the pioneer and perfecter of faith" (Heb 12:2, NIV). Newman admonishes, "Let us look [to] Him who alone can guide us to that better country."[294]

We need to try to see ourselves, Newman continues, "as sheep in the trackless desert, who, unless they follow the shepherd, will be sure to lose themselves, sure to fall in with the wolf."[295] We will be safe so long as "we keep close to [Christ], and under His eye; but if we suffer Satan to gain an advantage over us, woe to us!"[296] These remarks by Newman highlight our reliance upon God's grace. The journey of faith, as he indicates, is not a solo endeavor in which we heroically chart our own paths. Christ must be our guide. Unless we heed his voice, we will surely get lost. One of the leading causes of disciples' veering off course is human pride. We mistakenly think that we can go it alone, and we inevitably find ourselves in the ditch. In the Gospel of John, Our Lord warns against the mindset of self-reliance: "I am the vine, you are the branches. He who abides in me, and I in him, he it is that bears much fruit, for apart from me you can do nothing" (Jn 15:5).

Alongside an absolute reliance upon Jesus, we need to foster singularity of purpose. "The many," Newman observes, "walk without aim or object. ... They follow whatever strikes them and pleases them; they indulge their natural tastes."[297] No person in his right mind would begin a trip without a clear plan for getting to his destination, yet that is how we often approach our spiritual lives. "The many," Newman presses, "are hindered, nay, possessed and absorbed by this world. ... They have no treasure above, but their treasure, and their heart, and their faculties are all upon the earth; the earth is their portion, and not heaven."[298] Christ tells us forthrightly: "No one can serve two masters" (Mt 6:24). Do we take this admonition seriously, or do we go about life without aim or object, lunging at whatever happens to strike our fancy? If the latter, then the earth will be our portion, not heaven.

When we diagnose ourselves as having a divided heart, it can be tempting to seek out a quick and easy remedy. But nothing like that exists. The steps to new life require discipline and sacrifice. Newman gives several concrete directives, including (foundationally) to "live by [a] rule."[299] This rule will take on different forms for different persons, depending on their station in life. The important point is that we establish some rule of life, for we will never make any progress apart from setting goals. And as we go about discerning what kind of rule is best for us, the priority should be to give our best to God: "Set aside every day times for seeking Him ... not to give hours to mere amusement or society, while you give minutes to Christ; not to pray to Him only when you are tired, and fit for nothing but sleep; ... but in good measure to realize honestly the words of the text, to 'set your affection on things above.' "[300] These sorts of habits are essential. It is one thing to talk about dependence on God; it's quite another to live that way. Newman, with characteristic directness, gets to the crux of the matter: "Prayer and fasting have been called the wings of the soul, and they who neither fast nor pray, cannot follow Christ."[301] If we claim to be reliant upon grace but do not regularly fast and pray, our words are empty. By our actions we demonstrate where our trust resides.

LIVING IN THE LIGHT OF ETERNITY

Ultimately, John Henry Newman became a saint because he subordinated the temporal affairs of life to eternal concerns. That is to say, Newman prioritized his time and energies on the basis of what he believed would resound in eternity. At the end of his *Essay on the Development of Christian Doctrine*, for example, he closed the discussion by reminding his readers, "Time is short, eternity is long."[302] When we feel convicted by a sermon or a theological text, it can be easy to dismiss that prompting by convincing ourselves that we have other concerns that take priority. Newman saw how this could be the case for Anglicans, especially clergy, who felt drawn to the Catholic Church but worried that to take that final step would mean losing friendships, career prospects, and the esteem of their colleagues. So, in the essay where he set forth his most extensive case for the truth of the Catholic Faith, Newman gave a direct message to those who might be thinking in those terms: "Put not from you what you have here found; regard it not as mere matter of present controversy; set not out resolved to refute it, and looking about for the best way of doing so. ... Wrap not yourself round in the associations of years past, nor determine that to be truth which you wish to be so. ... Time is short, eternity is long."[303] If Catholicism is true, then the Church as representative of Christ commands our allegiance. None of our concerns about the loss of temporal goods matter in light of what is ultimately at stake.

This anxiety over temporal concerns is one that every generation of Christians must face. During Jesus' lifetime, those who heard his preaching gave all sorts of excuses as to why they could not follow him. The Gospel of Luke records some of these instances:

> As they were going along the road, a man said to him, "I will follow you wherever you go." And Jesus said to him, "Foxes have holes, and birds of the air have nests; but the Son of man has nowhere to lay his head." To another he said, "Follow me." But he said, "Lord, let me first go and bury my father." But he said to him, "Leave the dead to bury their own dead; but as for you, go and proclaim the kingdom of God." Another said, "I will follow you, Lord; but let me first say farewell to those at

> my home." Jesus said to him, "No one who puts
> his hand to the plow and looks back is fit for the
> kingdom of God" (Lk 9:57–62).

Evidently, some of the excuses given to Jesus were more legitimate than others. For instance, can we really fault a man for wanting to bury his father? According to the dictates of our own faith, this act is one of the corporal works of mercy and should be encouraged in most circumstances. Nevertheless, as the above passage shows, even good desires — wrongly ordered — can become obstacles that stand in the way of following God. Any good, if it is prioritized above our allegiance to God, risks becoming an idol. Time is short, eternity is long.

As we have seen, one serious challenge when it comes to heeding God's voice is that the things of this world are immediate to us and thus tend to draw our attention away from eternal realities. "Indeed, it is a very difficult thing to bring home to us, and to feel, that we have souls."[304] The multitude of Christians, in fact, don't realize it, at least not in a way that changes how they live their lives. Rather,

> a thick veil is drawn over their eyes; and in spite
> of their being able to talk of the [immortality of
> the soul], they [act] as if they never had heard
> of it. They go on just as the heathen did of old:
> they eat, they drink; or they amuse themselves in
> vanities, and live in the world, without fear and
> without sorrow, just as if God had not declared
> that their conduct in this life would decide their
> destiny in the next.[305]

Because we are sensory creatures, it's difficult for us sometimes to see beyond the goods of this world. Earthly realities appear so solid and substantial, the reality of eternal life so far away. Newman even goes so far as to say that "we never in this life can fully understand what is meant by our living forever."[306] Such an experience will be so drastically different from the life we now know that we can only begin to comprehend it by way of analogy.

What we *can* understand, Newman suggests, is "what is meant by this world's *not* living forever, by its dying never to rise again."[307] Through our basic experience of the world, we come to witness corruption and death. We know that biological organisms, whether plants or animals, do not live forever but inevitably deteriorate and die. If we take this fact of life and apply it more expansively, we can even imagine our own sun — impressive as it is — burning out and life on earth being no more. "And learning this, we learn that we owe [the world] no service, no allegiance; it has no claim over us, and can do us no material good nor harm."[308] This thought, on its own, gets us only halfway, though. We have to supplement our recognition of the world's futility with obedience to the law of God written on our hearts. This obedience begins for most of us with listening to the voice of conscience. A person of religious mind, Newman notes, is one "who attends to the rule of conscience, which is born with him, which he did not make for himself, and to which he feels bound in duty to submit."[309] Insofar as we heed the promptings of conscience, we will grow in our awareness of God's presence. For "conscience immediately directs [a person's] thoughts to some Being exterior to himself, who gave it, and who evidently is superior to him; for a law implies a lawgiver, and a command implies a superior."[310]

Now we see more clearly what Newman means when he says that "obedience to the light we possess is the way to gain more light."[311] As we listen to God's voice, mediated to us both by conscience and Scripture, we draw closer to God and are able to see the world for what it is — as God's good creation but also passing away and therefore not able to satisfy our deepest longings. "And thus [a person] is drawn forward by all manner of powerful influences to turn from things temporal to things eternal, to deny himself, to take up his cross and follow Christ."[312] The various factors that we have been discussing are converging influences on our perspective of reality. In the initial stages of the spiritual life, it's admittedly not easy to see beyond worldly things in order to fix our gaze on what is eternal, but there are steps we can take to break through this barrier. If we envision the temporality of the created order and combine that with a consistent obedience to the dictates of conscience, our vision will be sharpened and attuned to eternal realities. "They who, through grace, obey the secret voice of God, move onward contrary to the world's way," Newman writes. They become careless to what others "may say of them," and come to understand that they were designed for eternity, "which is the one thing they have to care about."[313]

In Ecclesiastes, chapter 3, we read that God has set eternity in the human heart. This verse reminds us that God has created us for eternity, a corollary of which is that no earthly good can satisfy the deepest longings of the human heart. As Newman puts it, "The thought of God, and nothing short of it, is the happiness of man."[314] This truth can prove difficult to embrace, particularly in a society fueled by consumerism and hedonism, in which there are so many distractions that vie for our attention. But, as Newman reminds us, it is simply irrational to give our hearts to things that "have no permanence in them."[315] Because our hearts were designed for eternity, the source of true happiness must be both lasting and also infinitely good and beautiful. The sooner we accept this truth — not in theory, but in practice — the quicker we will be on our way to authentic happiness. Even though he died over a century ago, Newman's counsel on all this remains as relevant now as it was when he first gave it:

> Life passes, riches fly away, popularity is fickle,
> the senses decay, the world changes, friends die.
> One alone is constant; One alone is true to us;
> One alone can be true; One alone can be all things
> to us; One alone can supply our needs; One alone

can train us up to our full perfection; One alone can give a meaning to our complex and intricate nature; One alone can give us tune and harmony; One alone can form and possess us. Are we allowed to put ourselves under His guidance? This surely is the only question. Has He really made us His children, and taken possession of us by His Holy Spirit? Are we still in His kingdom of grace, in spite of our sins? The question is not whether we should go, but whether He will receive. And we trust, that, in spite of our sins, He will receive us still, every one of us, if we seek His face in love unfeigned, and holy fear. Let us then do our part, as He has done His, and much more. Let us say with the Psalmist, "Whom have I in heaven but Thee? and there is none upon earth I desire in comparison of Thee. My flesh and my heart faileth; but God is the strength of my heart, and my portion forever."[316]

COR AD COR LOQUITUR

In the introduction to this volume, I made the following point, which is worth reiterating here: "Like Abraham, we have to be willing to journey to an unfamiliar place if we are to discover all that God has prepared for us to accomplish. If Newman's spiritual wisdom is going to bear fruit in your life, you must be willing to act on the convictions that well up within you before you necessarily see the whole picture." Briefly stated, if you or I were to master completely the content of Newman's theology but were to stop there, it would be a worthless exercise. The truths of the Faith that Newman conveys through his writings are not meant to be studied as useful trivia in preparation for Catholic *Jeopardy*. Rather, they are meant to be put into practice. Learning theology simply as an abstract intellectual endeavor would be like stockpiling life-saving medical supplies and then allowing them to rot in a warehouse.

We hear strong affirmations of this point in the Gospels, wherein Jesus challenges his followers to conduct themselves in such a way that their very existence becomes a living proclamation of God's love: "You are the light of the world. A city set on a hill cannot be hid. Nor do men light a lamp and put it under a bushel, but on a stand, and it gives light to all in the house. Let your light so shine before others, that they may see your good works and give glory to your Father who is in heaven" (Mt 5:14–16, slightly revised). A lamp is worthwhile only insofar as it provides light to those who need it; a lamp that remains hidden is, quite frankly, good for nothing. At another point in his teaching ministry, Jesus tells a parable that drives this point home. The kingdom of heaven, Jesus says, is like "a man going on a journey [who] call[s] his servants and entrust[s] to them his property" (Mt 25:14). In the parable, two of the servants invest the money they are given and are able to present the interest to the master upon his return. The third servant, in contrast, buries his talent in the ground, because he is afraid of losing what the master gave to him. Upon learning what this cautious servant has done, the master thunders,

> You wicked and slothful servant! You knew that
> I reap where I have not sowed, and gather where
> I have not winnowed? Then you ought to have
> invested my money with the bankers, and at my
> coming I should have received what was my own
> with interest. So take the talent from him, and
> give it to him who has the ten talents. For to every
> one who has will more be given, and he will have
> abundance; but from him who has not, even what
> he has will be taken away. (Mt 25:26–29)

When we protectively hoard the treasures and talents God has blessed us with, we may assume that we are somehow being prudent, even doing God a favor. But, as Jesus highlights in this parable, any gifts that we receive from God can accomplish the work that God intends only when they are shared with others. That is the return investment we should be seeking.

How does all of this apply to what we have been discussing in this book? Simple: Saint John Henry Newman did not write theological tomes to pad his resume or to display his considerable intellectual talents. No, Newman was centrally concerned about one thing: helping others to grow in their faith, so that they could know the full measure of God's love. Along these lines, in his sermon "Personal Influence, the Means of Propagating the Truth," Newman highlights that passing along the truths of the Faith cannot be reduced to a matter of using eloquent speech. The problem with such an approach, he says, is that revealed truths "cannot [adequately] be explained and defended in words," because ultimately the truths of the Faith "and human language are incommensurable."[317] Thus, what is needed in order to propagate the truth is for heroic persons to live in such a way that their words are wedded to sacrificial acts of love and mercy. As Newman points out, the Christian faith "has been upheld in the world not as a system, not by books, not by argument, nor by temporal power, but by the personal influence of such [persons] ... who are at once the teachers and the patterns of it."[318] Thus, "one little deed, done against natural inclination for God's sake ... to brook an insult, to face a danger, or to resign an advantage, has in it a power outbalancing all the dust and chaff of mere profession."[319] The way that all of this works might be described as the surprising math of the Gospel. We accomplish more in one small act of selflessness than any number of eloquent words, if these words are a "mere profession." Preaching the Gospel is vital, for sure, but words that do not translate into action amount to a dead letter.

In order to be faithful evangelizers, moreover, we have to go about this task with a clear understanding of the nature of Christian conversion. From Newman's vantage point, persons are not normally converted by syllogisms or other forms of rational argumentation. As he sees the matter, "The heart is commonly reached, not through the reason, but through the imagination. ... Persons influence us, voices melt us, looks subdue us, deeds inflame us. Many a man will live and die upon a dogma: no man will be a martyr for a conclusion."[320] In this respect, "logic makes but a sorry rhetoric with the multitude."[321] It's easier to shoot around corners, Newman asserts, than to argue others into the Faith, and adopting this tactic often proves counterproductive. "I do not want to be converted by a smart syllogism," he writes elsewhere; "if I am asked to convert others by it, I say plainly I do not care to overcome their reason without touching their hearts. I wish to deal not with controversialists, but with inquirers."[322] One can see a practical outcome of this perspective in the way that Newman approached his teaching. When the provost of Oriel College took steps to curtail his tutoring, Newman halted his teaching responsibilities altogether, because, for him, delivering information in a classroom without the personal influence that came with directly mentoring students made no sense.

Tellingly, when Pope Leo XIII honored Newman in 1879 by making him a cardinal, Newman chose as his cardinalitial motto the Latin phrase *Cor ad cor loquitur*, which means "Heart speaks to heart." Newman's engagement with the Church Fathers was a case of heart speaking to heart. Through the written word, these early Christian writers spoke to Newman's heart, and as a result, he chose to dedicate his life to serving Christ's Church by becoming a priest. Throughout his many years of priestly ministry, Newman touched the hearts of innumerable persons, and today his heart continues to speak to other hearts by virtue of the impressive body of writings that he left behind. Those of us who have been moved by Newman's legacy can best honor him by imitating his example of evangelism through personal influence. If Newman has helped you to move out of shadows and deeper into the truth, then I encourage you to go and do likewise in your daily interactions with others. Think of the impact on the world that we could have if we committed to walking together under the banner of *Cor ad cor loquitur,* trusting all the while that the Holy Spirit will go ahead of us to prepare the way. Finally, as we march together toward the heavenly Jerusalem, let us never forget that we are surrounded by a great cloud of witnesses, of which Newman is most certainly a member.

Saint John Henry Newman, pray for us.

ACKNOWLEDGMENTS

I owe a special debt of gratitude to my wife, Rachel, as her unflagging support and generous sacrifice of time make possible my research and writing efforts. Brother Reed Frey, CO, and Dave Capan graciously read earlier drafts of the manuscript of this book and provided feedback that substantially improved the text. Any shortcomings that remain, of course, belong only to me. Finally, the book is dedicated to Catharine M. Ryan and Father Drew Morgan, cofounders of the National Institute for Newman Studies. The world of Newman studies would not be what it is today without the many sacrifices that Catharine and Father Drew have made to help others learn about Saint John Henry Newman. Their devotion to Newman has been a source of inspiration to me, and apart from their vision and leadership, this book would have never come to fruition. Thank you both!

SELECTED BIBLIOGRAPHY

Aquinas, Thomas. *The Aquinas Prayer Book: The Prayers and Hymns of St. Thomas Aquinas*. Translated and edited by Robert Anderson and Johann Moser. Manchester, NH: Sophia Institute Press, 2000.

―――. *Commentary on Aristotle's* Politics. Edited by Richard Regan. Indianapolis: Hackett Publishing, 2007.

―――. *Summa Theologiae*. Translated by the Fathers of the English Dominican Province. Westminster, MD: Christian Classics, 1981.

Benedict XVI. Encyclical Letter *Spe Salvi* (November 30, 2007). Vatican.va.

Bobrinskoy, Boris. *The Mystery of the Trinity: Trinitarian Experience and Vision in the Biblical and Patristic Tradition*. Crestwood, NY: St. Vladimir's Seminary Press, 1999.

Butin, Philip W. *The Trinity*. Louisville, KY: Geneva Press, 2001.

Cornwell, John. *Newman's Unquiet Grave: The Reluctant Saint*. London: Continuum, 2011.

Ker, Ian. *The Achievement of John Henry Newman*. Notre Dame, IN: University of Notre Dame Press, 1990.

―――. *Healing the Wound of Humanity: The Spirituality of John Henry Newman*. London: Darton, Longman and Todd, 1993.

―――. *Newman on Being a Christian*. Notre Dame, IN: University of Notre Dame Press, 2000.

Kowalska, Saint Maria Faustina. *Diary: Divine Mercy in My Soul*, 3rd rev. ed. Stockbridge, MA: Marian Press, 2014.

Peter Kreeft. "What Is a Saint?," *National Catholic Register* (October 1987).

Lattier, Daniel. "John Henry Newman on Deification." In *Called to Be the Children of God: The Catholic Theology of Human Deification*, edited by David Meconi and Carl Olson, 181–97. San Francisco, CA: Ignatius Press, 2016.

Lewis, C. S. *The Voyage of the Dawn Treader*. New York: Collier Books, 1952.

————. *The Weight of Glory and Other Addresses*. New York: HarperOne, 2007.

Liguori, Alphonsus. *The Glories of Mary*. New York: Edward Dunigan & Brother, 1852.

Lubac, Henri de. *Catholicism: Christ and the Common Destiny of Man*. Translated by Lancelot C. Sheppard and Elizabeth Englund. San Francisco: Ignatius Press, 1988.

Martin, Ralph. *The Fulfillment of All Desire: A Guidebook for the Journey to God Based on the Wisdom of the Saints*. Steubenville, OH: Emmaus Road, 2006.

McInroy, Mark. "Before Deification Became Eastern: Newman's Ecumenical Retrieval." *International Journal for Systematic Theology* 20 (2018): 253–68.

Meconi, David. *The One Christ: St. Augustine's Theology of Deification*. Washington, DC: Catholic University of America Press, 2018.

Moleski, Martin X. *Personal Catholicism: The Theological Epistemologies of John Henry Newman and Michael Polanyi.* Washington, DC: Catholic University of America Press, 2001.

Newman, John Henry. *Apologia Pro Vita Sua: Being a History of His Religious Opinions.* Edited by Martin J. Svalgic. 1864–1865. Reprint, Oxford: Oxford University Press, 2016.

————. *An Essay on the Development of Christian Doctrine.* New Edition. London: Basil Montagu Pickering, 1878; reprint, London: Longmans, Green, and Co., 1909.

————. *Autobiographical Writings.* Edited by Henry Tristram. London: Sheed & Ward, 1968.

————. *Discourses Addressed to Mixed Congregations.* London: Longmans, 1849. Reprint, Notre Dame, IN: University of Notre Dame Press, 2003.

————. *Discussions and Arguments on Various Subjects.* London: Basil Montegu Pickering, 1872. Reprint, Notre Dame, IN: University of Notre Dame Press, 2004.

————. *An Essay in Aid of a Grammar of Assent.* London: Burns, Oates, 1870. Reprint, Notre Dame, IN: University of Notre Dame Press, 2003.

————. *Essays, Critical and Historical.* London: B. M. Pickering, 1871.

————. *Fifteen Sermons Preached before the University of Oxford between A.D. 1826 and 1843.* London: Rivingtons, 1890.

————. *Lectures on the Doctrine of Justification.* New York: Scribner, Welford, and Armstrong, 1874.

————. *Lectures on the Present Position of Catholics in England: Addressed to the Brothers of the Oratory in the Summer of 1851.* London: Burns & Lambert, 1851. Reprint, Notre Dame, IN: University of Notre Dame Press, 2000.

————. *The Letters and Diaries of John Henry Newman.* Edited by Charles Stephen Dessain et al. Vols. i–vi. Oxford: Clarendon Press, 1978–1984.

————. *The Letters and Diaries of John Henry Newman.* Edited by Charles Stephen Dessain et al. Vols. xi–xxii. London: Nelson, 1961–1972.

————. *The Letters and Diaries of John Henry Newman.* Edited by Charles Stephen Dessain et al. Vols. xxiii–xxxi. Oxford: Clarendon Press, 1973–1977.

————. *Meditations and Devotions of the Late Cardinal Newman.* Edited by W. P. Neville. London: Longmans, Green, 1893.

————. *Parochial and Plain Sermons.* 8 vols. Edited by W. J. Copeland. London: Rivingtons, 1868. Reprint, Westminster, MD: Christian Classics, 1968.

————. *Sayings of Cardinal Newman.* Edited by anonymous. London: Burns & Oates, 1890.

————. *Sermons Bearing on Subjects of the Day.* London: Rivingtons, 1869.

————. *Sermons Preached on Various Occasions.* London: Burns and Oates, 1870. Reprint, Notre Dame, IN: University of Notre Dame Press, 2007.

————. *Verses on Various Occasions.* London: Burns, Oates & Washbourne, 1867.

Oakes, Edward. *Infinity Dwindled to Infancy: A Catholic and Evangelical Christology.* Grand Rapids, MI: Eerdmans, 2011.

Paul VI. *Acta Apostolicae Sedis.* Annus 50, series 3. Vol. 5 of *Commentarium Officiale.* Città del Vaticano: Typis Polyglottis Vaticanis, 1963.

Strange, Roderick. *Newman 101.* Notre Dame, IN: Christian Classics, 2008.

Ward, Wilfrid. *The Life of John Henry, Cardinal Newman: Based on His Private Journals and Correspondence.* Vol. 1. New York: Longmans, Green, 1912.

Wilson, Bishop Thomas. *Sacra Privata: The Private Meditations and Prayers of the Right Reverend Thomas Wilson, D.D., Lord Bishop of Sodor and Man, Accommodated to General Use.* Andover, MA: Flagg and Gould, 1819.

Winterton, Gregory. Introduction to *The Dream of Gerontius,* by John Henry Newman, 3–15, Oxford: Family Publications, 2001.

NOTES

INTRODUCTION: NEWMAN AS SPIRITUAL GUIDE ON THE PATH TO HOLINESS

1. Saint Maria Faustina Kowalska, *Diary: Divine Mercy in My Soul*, 3rd rev. ed. (Stockbridge, MA: Marian Press, 2014), no. 35.

2. Ibid., no. 331.

3. John Henry Newman, *Sermons Bearing on Subjects of the Day* (London: Rivingtons, 1869), 48–49. Hereafter cited as *SD*.

4. John Henry Newman, *Discourses Addressed to Mixed Congregations* (London: Longmans, 1849; repr., Notre Dame, IN: University of Notre Dame Press, 2003), 108. Hereafter cited as *Mix.*

5. *Mix.*, 108.

6. John Henry Newman, *Discussions and Arguments on Various Subjects* (London: Basil Montegu Pickering, 1872; repr., Notre Dame, IN: University of Notre Dame Press, 2004), 295. Hereafter cited as *DA*.

7. John Henry Newman, *Apologia Pro Vita Sua: Being a History of His Religious Opinions*, ed. Martin J. Svalgic (1864–1865; repr., Oxford: Oxford University Press, 2016), 239. Hereafter cited as *Apo.*

8. John Henry Newman. *Parochial and Plain Sermons*, ed. W. J. Copeland, 8 vols. (London: Rivingtons, 1868; repr., Westminster, MD: Christian Classics, 1968), iv. 296. Hereafter cited as *PS*, with citations specified by volume and page number.

9. *PS* iv. 296.

10. John Henry Newman, *Lectures on the Present Position of Catholics in England: Addressed to the Brothers of the Oratory in the Summer of 1851* (London: Burns & Lambert, 1851; repr., Notre Dame, IN: University of Notre Dame Press, 2000), 403.

11. A graduate-school professor of mine humorously captured this outlook with a bumper sticker on his car. It simply

read, "Jesus loves you; everyone else thinks you're a jerk."

12. *PS* iv. 306.

13. *PS* iv. 306.

14. *PS* v. 210.

15. John Henry Newman, *Meditations and Devotions of the Late Cardinal Newman*, ed. W. P. Neville (London: Longmans, Green, 1893). Hereafter cited as *MD*. The complete work is available online at http://www.newmanreader.org/works/meditations/index.html.

16. *SD*, 307.

1. Highlights from Newman's Life

17. Paul VI, *Acta Apostolicae Sedis*, annus 50, series 3, vol. 5 of *Commentarium Officiale* (Vatican City: Typis Polyglottis Vaticanis, 1963), 1025, accessed May 27, 2020, http://www.vatican.va/archive/aas/documents/AAS-55-1963-ocr.pdf.

18. John Henry Newman, *An Essay in Aid of a Grammar of Assent* (London: Burns, Oates, 1870; repr., Notre Dame, IN: University of Notre Dame Press, 2003), 56. Hereafter cited as *GA*.

19. John Henry Newman, *Autobiographical Writings*, ed. Henry Tristram (London: Sheed & Ward, 1968), 63. Hereafter cited as *AW*.

20. Since Newman considered Lutheranism heretical, he could not countenance the idea of sharing episcopal authority with Lutherans. If the Church of England was truly Catholic, as it claimed to be, how could it be in communion with a heretical sect?

21. *Apo.*, 245.

22. *Apo.*, 238.

23. *The Letters and Diaries of John Henry Newman*, ed. Charles Stephen Dessain et al., vols. i–vi (Oxford: Clarendon Press, 1978–1984); vols. xi–xxii (London: Nelson, 1961–1972); vols. xxiii–xxxi (Oxford: Clarendon Press, 1973–1977); xx. 215–16. Hereafter cited as *LD*, with citations specified by volume and page number.

24. *LD* xxv. 310 (emphasis added).

25. See, for example, Newman's letter to William George Ward, dated 9 May 1867: "Pardon me if I say you are making a Church within a Church, as the Novatians of old did. ... You are doing your best to make a party in the Catholic Church, and in Saint Paul's words are '*dividing Christ*' by exalting your opinions into dogmas, and shocking to say, by declaring to me, as you do, that those Catholics who do not accept them are of a different religion from yours. I protest then again, not against your tenets, but against what I must call your schismatical spirit. I disown your intended praise of me viz that I hold your theological opinions 'in the greatest aversion,' and I pray God that I may never denounce, as you do, what the Church has not denounced." *LD* xxiii. 217 (emphasis in the original).

26. *PS* ii. 54.

27. *PS* ii. 60.

28. Collect for October 9, the feast of Saint John Henry Newman.

2. THE THREE STAGES OF THE SPIRITUAL LIFE

29. I emphasize the liturgical life here, rather than doctrine or moral laws (important as they are), because the liturgy is the natural context in which we are meant to hear and receive God's Word.

30. One of the best recent treatments of this threefold path of discipleship is Ralph Martin, *The Fulfillment of All Desire: A Guidebook for the Journey to God Based on the Wisdom of the Saints* (Steubenville, OH: Emmaus Road, 2006).

31. *PS* v. 242. Full quotation: "They wish to be saved, but in their own way; they wish (as it were) to capitulate upon terms, to carry off their goods with them; whereas the true spirit of faith leads a man to look off from self to God, to think nothing of his own wishes, his present habits, his importance or dignity, his rights, his opinions, but to say, 'I put myself into Thy hands, O Lord; make Thou me what Thou wilt; I forget myself; I divorce

myself from myself; I am dead to myself; I will follow Thee.' "

32. *PS* v. 241.

33. Cf. *PS* v. 343: "The only qualification which will avail us for heaven is the love of God. We may keep from gross sinning, and yet not have this divine gift, 'without which we are dead' in God's sight. *This changes our whole being;* this makes us live; this makes us grow in grace and abound in good works; *this makes us fit for God's presence hereafter*" (emphasis added).

34. *PS* v. 210.

35. Cf. *MD*, 285: "It is the saying of holy men that, if we wish to be perfect, we have nothing more to do than to perform the ordinary duties of the day well. A short road to perfection — short, not because easy, but because pertinent and intelligible. There are no short ways to perfection, but there are sure ones."

36. *PS* i. 252.

37. Ian Ker, *The Achievement of John Henry Newman* (Notre Dame, IN: University of Notre Dame Press, 1990), 76.

38. *PS* vii. 100–1.

39. *PS* iii. 144.

40. *PS* iii. 139.

41. In this instance, I quote the verse as it is cited in Newman's sermon. During his Anglican period, Newman preached from the King James Bible, as was customary.

42. *PS* iii. 142 (emphasis in the original).

43. *PS* iii. 142.

44. *PS* iii. 151.

45. *PS* i. 70.

46. *PS* i. 70.

47. *PS* i. 70.

48. *PS* i. 57.

49. *PS* vii. 65.

50. *PS* vii. 98 (emphasis added).

51. *PS* iii. 152. The quotation is of Bishop Thomas Wilson (1663–1755), *Sacra Privata: The Private Meditations and Prayers of the Right Reverend Thomas Wilson, D.D., Lord Bishop of Sodor*

and Man, Accommodated to General Use (New York: D. Appleton & Co., 1841), 140.

52. *PS* ii. 347–48.

53. *PS* ii. 348.

54. *PS* ii. 345.

55. *PS* ii. 344.

56. *PS* ii. 346.

57. King James Version (KJV), as quoted in Newman's sermon.

58. In Newman's words, "Whatever be the line of conduct [these passages] prescribe to this or that individual …, so far seems clear, that according to the rule of the Gospel, the absence of wealth is, as such, a more blessed and a more Christian state than the possession of it." Cf. *PS* ii. 347.

59. *PS* ii. 347.

60. *PS* ii. 347.

61. Cf. the *Baltimore Catechism*, no. 1, q. 6.

62. *PS* ii. 349 (emphasis in the original).

63. *PS* ii. 353.

64. *PS* ii. 354.

65. Cf. Thomas Aquinas, *Summa Theologiae* II-II, q. 66, a. 1–2; Thomas Aquinas, *Commentary on Aristotle's* Politics, ed. Richard Regan (Indianapolis: Hackett Publishing, 2007), bk. 1, chap. 6.

66. Cf. Newman, *PS* ii. 353–54: "You may hear men talk as if the pursuit of wealth was the business of life. They will argue, that by the law of nature a man is bound to gain a livelihood for his family, and that he finds a reward in doing so, an innocent and honorable satisfaction, as he adds one sum to another, and counts up his gains. And perhaps they go on to argue, that it is the very duty of man since Adam's fall, 'in the sweat of his face,' by effort and anxiety, 'to eat bread.' How strange it is that they do not remember Christ's gracious promise, repealing that original curse, and obviating the necessity of any real pursuit after 'the meat that perisheth!' "

67. One final word on this topic: It's worth noting that

the sermon I have highlighted above constitutes Newman's harshest word that he preached regarding the topic of wealth. As Newman continued in his ministry, he came to recognize over time that he could not do the work that God had prepared him apart from the generosity of benefactors with means. At one point, Newman even paid for an advertisement that highlighted the duty of the rich to provide for the material fabric of divine worship — i.e., the beautification of churches — so it's clear that he saw a crucial role for such persons in the life of the body of Christ. I include this qualification not to slacken the radicality of Jesus' teachings, but simply to acknowledge that the Church, historically, has been made up of both the poor and the well-to-do. Yes, the wealthy bear a special burden (to whom much is given, much is expected, etc.), but the strong admonitions that Scripture gives on such matters should not be interpreted to mean that the rich are, in principle, excluded from the kingdom of heaven. In fact, when Jesus gives his famous saying about it being easier for a camel to pass through the eye of a needle than for a rich person to be saved, the disciples respond by asking, "Who then can be saved?" Upon hearing their question, Jesus offers the quick rejoinder, "With men this is impossible, but with God all things are possible" (Mt 19:25–26). Whenever we discuss these matters, then, we ought to do so with due charity, not being envious of how God has chosen to bless others, and concerning ourselves primarily with the question of how we have stewarded the specific material blessings that God has showered upon us. In reality, each one of us — if left to our own devices — would be lost. In that sense, the salvation of each individual person is a result of God making the impossible possible.

68. These definitions are taken from Martin X. Moleski, *Personal Catholicism: The Theological Epistemologies of John Henry Newman and Michael Polanyi* (Washington, DC: Catholic University of America Press, 2001), 20.

69. *PS* v. 317–18.
70. *PS* v. 318.
71. *PS* v. 318.
72. *PS* v. 324–25.
73. *PS* v. 319.
74. *PS* v. 10.
75. *PS* v. 10–11.
76. *PS* i. 4–5 (emphasis in the original).
77. *PS* i. 5 (emphasis in the original).
78. *PS* i. 6–7.
79. *PS* i. 7.
80. Cf. *Mix.*, 169: "And, again, when God, for Christ's sake, is about to restore any one to His favor, His first act of mercy is to impart to [that person] a portion of this grace; the first-fruits of that sovereign, energetic power, which forms and harmonizes his whole nature, and enables it to fulfil its own end, while it fulfils one higher than its own."
81. *Mix.*, 168.
82. *PS* iv. 200.
83. *PS* iv. 200.
84. *PS* iv. 202.
85. *PS* iv. 205.
86. *PS* iv. 209.
87. *PS* iv. 210.
88. *PS* iv. 211.
89. *PS* iv. 211–13.
90. *PS* iv. 198.

3. Learning the New Language of Christ

91. *PS* v. 44.
92. Saint Thomas Aquinas, *The Aquinas Prayer Book: The Prayers and Hymns of St. Thomas Aquinas*, trans. and ed. Robert Anderson and Johann Moser (Manchester, NH: Sophia Institute Press, 2000), 41–43.
93. *PS* i. 66.

94. *PS* i. 66 (emphasis added).

95. *PS* i. 39.

96. *PS* i. 39.

97. *PS* i. 37.

98. *PS* i. 37 (emphasis in the original).

99. *PS* i. 38.

100. *PS* i. 67.

101. *LD* xi. 191.

102. Ian Ker, *Newman on Being a Christian* (Notre Dame, IN: University of Notre Dame Press, 2000), 119.

103. Cf. *PS* i. 30.

104. *PS* i. 172.

105. *PS* vii. 100–1.

106. *PS* i. 67.

107. *PS* vi. 34.

108. *PS* viii. 98.

109. *PS* i. 309.

110. *PS* v. 271.

111. *PS* v. 271.

112. *PS* v. 271.

113. *PS* viii. 254–55.

114. *Mix.*, 97.

115. *Mix.*, 97.

116. *Mix.*, 97.

117. *Mix.*, 98.

118. *Mix.*, 98.

119. *Mix.*, 99.

120. *Mix.*, 98.

121. *Mix.*, 376.

122. Quoted in Peter Kreeft, "What Is a Saint?" *National Catholic Register* (October 1987).

4. SALVATION AND THE INDWELLING OF THE HOLY SPIRIT

123. *MD*, 29–30.

124. *PS* vi. 41.

125. *PS* v. 241.

126. Homily of His Holiness Pope Benedict XVI, April 24, 2005, St. Peter's Square, accessed May 27, 2020, Vatican.va.

127. *PS* v. 241.

128. C. S. Lewis, *The Voyage of the Dawn Treader* (New York: Collier Books, 1952), 90–91.

129. Some recent Catholic scholarship has sought to recover the notion of *theosis*, showing that it has a venerable place in the Western tradition as well — for example, in the theology of Augustine. See, e.g., David Meconi, *The One Christ: St. Augustine's Theology of Deification* (Washington, DC: Catholic University of America Press, 2018). Mark McInroy argues that Newman played a crucial role in reintegrating this doctrine into Western theological discourse. Mark McInroy, "Before Deification Became Eastern: Newman's Ecumenical Retrieval," *International Journal for Systematic Theology* 20 (2018): 253–68. For a detailed overview of Newman's approach, see Daniel Lattier, "John Henry Newman on Deification," in *Called to Be the Children of God: The Catholic Theology of Human Deification*, ed. David Meconi and Carl Olson (San Francisco, CA: Ignatius Press, 2016), 181–97.

130. John Henry Newman, *Lectures on the Doctrine of Justification* (New York: Scribner, Welford, and Armstrong, 1874), 136. Hereafter cited as *Jfc.*

131. *Jfc.*, 138.

132. *Jfc.*, 137.

133. Cf. Philip W. Butin, *The Trinity* (Louisville, KY: Geneva Press, 2001), 35; Boris Bobrinskoy, *The Mystery of the Trinity: Trinitarian Experience and Vision in the Biblical and Patristic Tradition* (Crestwood, NY: St. Vladimir's Seminary Press, 1999), 21ff.

134. This prayer for the sending of the Holy Spirit has traditionally been referred to as the *epiclesis*.

135. *Jfc.*, 98.

136. *Jfc.*, 81.

137. *Jfc.*, 81.

138. *Jfc.*, 65.

139. *Jfc.*, 99.

140. *Jfc.*, 78.

141. Second Vatican Council, Dogmatic Constitution on the Church *Lumen Gentium*, accessed May 26, 2020, Vatican. va, par. 48.

142. *MD*, 336.

143. *MD*, 403–4.

144. *MD*, 340.

145. *MD*, 341.

146. *MD*, 401–2.

147. *MD*, 403.

148. *Mix.*, 124.

149. *Mix.*, 125.

150. *Mix.*, 126.

151. *Mix.*, 126.

152. *Mix.*, 126–27.

153. *Mix.*, 130.

154. *Mix.*, 143.

155. *Mix.*, 144.

156. John Henry Newman, *Sayings of Cardinal Newman*, ed. anonymous (London: Burns & Oates, 1890), 44.

157. Saint Alphonsus Liguori, *The Glories of Mary* (New York: Edward Dunigan & Brother, 1852), 195.

5. Fixing Our Eyes on Jesus

158. *PS* ii. 163.

159. *PS* ii. 167.

160. *PS* ii. 169.

161. See Ian Ker's discussion in *Healing the Wound of Humanity: The Spirituality of John Henry Newman* (London: Darton, Longman and Todd, 1993), 24–25.

162. *PS* iii. 130.

163. *PS* iii. 130–31.

164. John Henry Newman, *An Essay on the Development of Christian Doctrine*, new edition (London: Basil Montagu Pickering, 1878; reprint, London: Longmans, Green, and Co., 1909), 324. Hereafter cited as *Dev.*

165. *Mix.*, 323.

166. *LD* ii. 308.

167. *PS* vi. 74.

168. *PS* vi. 74.

169. See Newman's sermon in *Mix.*, 284–304.

170. John Henry Newman, *Sermons Preached on Various Occasions* (London: Burns and Oates, 1870; repr., Notre Dame, IN: University of Notre Dame Press, 2007), 81. Hereafter cited as *OS.*

171. Adapted from the title of Edward Oakes's book *Infinity Dwindled to Infancy: A Catholic and Evangelical Christology* (Grand Rapids, MI: Eerdmans, 2011).

172. *OS*, 81.

173. *OS*, 87.

174. *OS*, 85 (emphasis added).

175. *OS*, 86–87.

176. *OS*, 87.

177. *OS*, 88.

178. *OS*, 88.

179. *PS* vi. 70.

180. *PS* vi. 71.

181. *PS* vi. 89.

182. *PS* vi. 89.

183. *PS* vi. 89.

184. *PS* vi. 89.

185. *PS* vi. 90.

186. *PS* iii. 169.

187. PS iii. 169–70.

188. *PS* ii. 374.

189. *PS* vi. 80.

190. *OS*, 89–90.

6. NEWMAN ON PRAYER

191. *PS* vi. 208.

192. *PS* iv. 227.

193. *PS* vii. 209.

194. *PS* vii. 206.

195. Cf. *PS* i. 244–56.

196. *PS* vi. 220.

197. *PS* vii. 101.

198. See *PS* i. 257–70.

199. *PS* i. 258.

200. *PS* i. 261 (emphasis in the original).

201. *PS* i. 261 (emphasis in the original).

202. *PS* i. 261.

203. *PS* i. 263.

204. *PS* i. 263.

205. *PS* i. 263.

206. *PS* i. 264.

207. *PS* i. 264.

208. *PS* i. 266.

209. *PS* i. 269–70.

210. *PS* i. 270.

211. *PS* vii. 211.

212. *PS* vii. 211.

213. *PS* v. 4.

214. *PS* v. 2.

215. KJV, as quoted in Newman's sermon (emphasis in the original).

216. *PS* vii. 211–12.

217. *PS* iv. 331–32.

218. *PS* iv. 332.

219. *PS* iv. 332.

220. *PS* iv. 332.

221. *PS* iv. 332.

222. *PS* iv. 333.

7. A Good Death

223. *PS* vii. 3.

224. *Mix.*, 70.

225. *PS* vii. 7.

226. *PS* vii. 6.

227. *PS* vii. 10–11.

228. *PS* vii. 12.

229. *Mix.*, 105.

230. *Mix.*, 105–6.

231. *PS* v. 44: "Poor men and rich men, governors and governed, prosperous and discontented, learned and unlearned, each has his own way of looking at the things which come before him, and each has a wrong way. There is but one right way; it is the way in which God looks at the world. Aim at looking at it in God's way. Aim at seeing things as God sees them. Aim at forming judgments about persons, events, ranks, fortunes, changes, objects, such as God forms. Aim at looking at this life as God looks at it. Aim at looking at the life to come, and the world unseen, as God does. Aim at 'seeing the King in his beauty.' All things that we see are but shadows to us and delusions, unless we enter into what they really mean."

232. *PS* iv. 80–81.

233. *PS* iv. 82.

234. *PS* iv. 83

235. *PS* i. 17.

236. *PS* i. 17–18.

237. *PS* i. 18.

238. *PS* iv. 87.

239. *PS* iv. 86.

240. *PS* iv. 87.

241. *PS* iv. 91.

242. C. S. Lewis, *The Weight of Glory and Other Addresses* (New York: HarperOne, 2007), 45–46.

243. Ibid., 46.

244. *PS* iv. 92.

245. *Mix.*, 105. Cf. *PS* v. 337: "If I must, before conclud-

ing, remark upon the mode of overcoming the evil, I must say plainly this, that, fanciful though it may appear at first sight to say so, the comforts of life are the main cause of it; and, much as we may lament and struggle against it, till we learn to dispense with them in good measure, we shall not overcome it. Till we, in a certain sense, detach ourselves from our bodies, our minds will not be in a state to receive divine impressions, and to exert heavenly aspirations. A smooth and easy life an uninterrupted enjoyment of the goods of providence, full meals, soft raiment, well-furnished homes, the pleasure of sense, the feeling of security, the consciousness of wealth — these and the life, if we are not careful, choke up all the avenues of the soul through which the light and breath of heaven might come to us."

246. *LD* ii. 69.

247. *Apo.*, 128.

248. *PS* i. 17–18.

249. *Apo.*, 4.

250. See, e.g., Henri de Lubac, *Catholicism: Christ and the Common Destiny of Man*, trans. Lancelot C. Sheppard and Elizabeth Englund (San Francisco: Ignatius Press, 1988).

251. *PS* i. 20.

252. *PS* i. 98.

253. *PS* i. 19.

254. I am indebted to Roderick Strange for seeing how Newman's illness in Sicily shaped his understanding of providence. See Roderick Strange, *Newman 101* (Notre Dame, IN: Christian Classics, 2008), 109–22.

255. Cf. *LD* iv. 8: "I came to think that there was some willfulness in my coming to Sicily, as I did. ... And then I felt more than I had done the willfulness of my character generally. ... And then I recollected that the very day before I left Oxford, I had preached a University Sermon against willfulness, so that I seemed to have been predicting my own condemnation."

256. *AW*, 121.

257. John Henry Newman, *Verses on Various Occasions* (London: Burns, Oates & Washbourne, 1867), 156. Hereafter cited as *VV.*

258. *Mix.*, 105.

259. *PS* v. 313ff.

260. *MD*, 301–2.

261. John Henry Newman, *Essays, Critical and Historical* (London: B. M. Pickering, 1871), ii. 192. Hereafter cited as *Ess.*

262. *Ess.* ii. 193.

263. See the remarks by Gregory Winterton in his introduction to *The Dream of Gerontius* (Oxford: Family Publications, 2001), 4.

264. Strange, *Newman 101*, 152.

265. Ibid., 154.

266. *VV,* 323.

267. *VV,* 323.

268. *VV,* 324.

269. *VV,* 328.

270. *VV,* 328.

271. *VV,* 327 (emphasis added).

272. John Cornwell, *Newman's Unquiet Grave: The Reluctant Saint* (London: Continuum, 2011), 179.

273. *VV,* 332.

274. *VV,* 334–35.

275. *VV,* 366.

276. *VV,* 360.

277. *VV,* 367.

278. *VV,* 369.

279. *VV,* 370.

280. *VV,* 341.

281. Benedict XVI, *Spe Salvi*, accessed May 27, 2020, Vatican.va, no. 47.

EPILOGUE: LOVE, THE SEED OF HOLINESS

282. *PS* iv. 311.

283. *PS* iv. 318.

284. *PS* iv. 168.

285. *PS* iv. 325.

286. *SD*, 278–79.

287. *PS* v. 241.

288. *PS* v. 239–40, 242.

289. *PS* v. 252–53.

290. *PS* v. 241–42.

291. *PS* v. 242.

292. *PS* viii. 225.

293. *PS* viii. 242.

294. *PS* viii. 242.

295. *PS* viii. 242.

296. *PS* viii. 242–43.

297. *PS* vi. 209.

298. *PS* vi. 208–9.

299. *PS* vi. 220.

300. *PS* vi. 220.

301. *PS* vi. 208.

302. *Dev.*, 445.

303. *Dev.*, 445.

304. *PS* i. 17.

305. *PS* i. 18.

306. *PS* i. 21.

307. *PS* i. 21.

308. *PS* i. 21.

309. *PS* ii. 18.

310. *PS* ii. 18.

311. *PS* viii. 210.

312. *PS* i. 22.

313. *PS* i. 22.

314. *PS* v. 316.

315. *PS* v. 317.

316. *PS* v. 326.

317. John Henry Newman, *Fifteen Sermons Preached before the University of Oxford between A.D. 1826 and 1843* (London:

Rivingtons, 1890), 84. Hereafter cited as *US*.
318. *US*, 91–92.
319. *US*, 93
320. *DA*, 293.
321. *DA*, 294.
322. *GA*, 425.

About the Author

D r. Ryan "Bud" Marr (Ph.D., Saint Louis University) is director of the National Institute for Newman Studies and associate editor of the *Newman Studies Journal*. He is the author of *To Be Perfect Is to Have Changed Often*, on Newman's theology of the Church, and he has contributed essays to *Newman and Life in the Spirit*, *Learning from All the Faithful*, and *The Oxford Handbook of John Henry Newman*. Bud, his wife, Rachel, and their seven children reside in Pittsburgh, Pennsylvania.